SAFETY NET

SAFETY NET

THE STRATEGY FOR DE-RISKING YOUR INVESTMENTS
IN A TIME OF TURBULENCE

JAMES K. GLASSMAN

CROWN
BUSINESS

NEW YORK

Copyright © 2011 by James K. Glassman

All rights reserved.
Published in the United States by Crown Business,
an imprint of the Crown Publishing Group,
a division of Random House, Inc., New York.
www.crownpublishing.com

Crown Business is a registered trademark and the Crown Business
colophon is a trademark of Random House, Inc.

Library of Congress Cataloging-in-Publication Data
Glassman, James K.
Safety net : the strategy for de-risking your investments
in turbulent times / James K. Glassman. —1st ed.
p.   cm.
1. Stocks. 2. Investments. 3. Financial risk management.
4. Portfolio management. 5. Finance, Personal. I. Title.
HG6041.G537 2011
332.63'2—dc22   2010039436

ISBN 978-0-307-59126-5
eISBN 978-0-307-59127-2

PRINTED IN THE UNITED STATES OF AMERICA

Book design by Gretchen Achilles
Illustrations by Lynn Carruthers
Jacket design and art by W. G. Cookman

1   3   5   7   9   10   8   6   4   2

FIRST EDITION

To my father, Stanley Glassman
(1923–2005)

CONTENTS

*Understanding that we do not know the future is
such a simple statement, but it's so important.*

PETER L. BERNSTEIN (1919–2009)

SAFETY NET

May 12, 2019 01:02

39065147460628   03/Jun/2019
A wealth of common sense : why simplicity
trumps complexity in any investment plan
(CheckOut)

39065110483730   03/Jun/2019
Safety net : the strategy for de-risking your
investments in turbulent times (CheckOut)

Total   2 Item(s)

Fish Creek Library
Self Checkout
September,30,2016 16.04

39065123711903   10/21/2016
The professional financial advisor III
: putting transparency and integrity fi
rst

39065120341613   10/21/2016
This I believe : life lessons

39065110483730   10/21/2016
Safety net : the strategy for de-riskin
g your investments in turbulent times

Total   **3 item(s)**

You have 0 item(s) ready for pickup

To check your card and renew items

go to www.calgarylibrary.ca

or call 403-262-2928

INTRODUCTION

A MARGIN OF SAFETY FOR
THE RISK-AVERSE INVESTOR

What do investors want?

Solid gains and real security. To achieve both, you need to make changes in the way you invest, adapting to a world that itself has changed profoundly in the past decade. Consider the strategy laid out in this book as your safety net for an investing environment that's gotten much, much riskier because the world has gotten much, much riskier. It's not hard to make a list: 9/11, the sudden and unprecedented collapse of home values, the "flash crash" of May 2010, the BP oil blowout, the shutdown of European air traffic for weeks by an ash cloud, and many more, including, of course, the 2008–2009 catastrophe in the markets.

For years, investors were told that, while stocks might be rocky in the short run, they offered outstanding profits in the long run. The more stocks you owned, the better.

Investors were told that the U.S. economy had entered a new era of prosperity and that a new "investor class" of small shareholders would reap the benefits through their IRAs and 401(k) plans.

Instead, the first decade of the twenty-first century turned out to be the worst in history for stocks. Investors who practiced the strategies preached by nearly every seemingly responsible financial advisor saw their nest eggs cracked and crushed.

If you're like many investors, your response to the turmoil was either to opt out or to turn away—to ignore what was going on because it was just too painful to watch. As stock prices began to rise again, you might have crept back into the stock market—or bought gold or foreign currencies. But even if you summoned the courage to invest in stocks again, you did so with a distinct lack of confidence. You're worried that it could all happen again.

And you should be worried. It *will*.

As an investor today, you are probably confused, frightened, and downright disgusted. You want a solution to your investing troubles. You can find a solution—but only if you come to terms with changes in the world. The biggest change is that the world is far riskier than it was in the late twentieth century. That fact, however, is no reason for despair.

This book tells you exactly what's changed and how you can adjust. It does not offer a quick fix, a panicky prescription. Instead, it recommends a calm, reasoned approach—an antidote to fear. I demonstrate how, as an investor, you will succeed—with eyes wide open and with faith in the future of your own nest egg.

STOP INSISTING THAT THE OLD RULES APPLY

For three decades, I provided small investors with advice and moral support. I wrote financial columns for the *Washington Post, Reader's Digest,* and *Kiplinger's Personal Finance.* I appeared on CNBC, CNN, and ABC. I wrote two books. I testified before Congress. I talked with the biggest brains of Wall Street and academia. A student of history, I extolled the virtues of what worked in the past: no-nonsense, long-term investments in lots and lots of U.S. stocks.

I thought I understood investing. Painfully, however, I learned more about the subject in the past three years than in the past thirty. And I decided that it was time to stop insisting that the Old Rulebook still applied. It was time, I concluded, to tear it up and write one that fits the new era and the new facts.

This is a bold statement from someone who helped *write* the Old Rulebook.

In 1999, I coauthored a bestseller called *Dow 36,000.* It was a meticulously documented book, drawing on more than 200 years of financial history. While the book had a provocative title, its thesis was definitely mainstream. I argued that, because of what history indicated were their high returns and relatively low risk over the long term, shares of American companies were the best place to put your retirement money. Yes, stocks bounced up and down, but your job as an investor was to hang on and collect your reward for perseverance at the end.

I advocated the same strategy of heavy and diversified U.S. equity holdings that most sensible advisors espoused—but with an extra dollop of optimism.

And I was wrong.

As I write today, in December 2010, the Dow Jones Industrial Average is only about 20 percent higher than it was in January 1999, when I wrote the book, and nearly 3,000 points lower than at its peak in 2007. Even with dividends, your returns over the last decade have been only a few measly percentage points a year—instead of the nearly 10 percent that had been the historic norm since the mid-1920s.

Accounting for inflation, the ten-year period ending in early 2009 was the worst in recorded stock market history—worse than the decade of the Great Depression. I believe that my reading of the facts in the years I wrote a column for the *Washington Post* (and the book) was accurate and conscientious. But the facts *changed*. And, as economist John Maynard Keynes once said, "When the facts change, I change my mind. What do you do, sir?"

The changed facts have led me to a strategy that I call the "Margin of Safety." Its aim is to lower your risks while still producing solid profits. It's a strategy that fits the new era of investing—a time of both danger and opportunity.

It's also a strategy that recognizes reality. Whatever the decades of data show, investors will always approach stocks with a certain caution—as they should. Ronald Reagan once said that an economist was someone who watched something work in practice, and "wondered if it would work in theory." Well, in practice, stocks have been crushed—not just in 2008–2009 but at other times in history. In theory, the averages show that stocks are a good buy if you can hang on through the miserable periods, but most investors find that hard to do. Fear (or simply a need for cash) triumphs, and they sell before stocks bounce back. For them, the Margin of Safety strategy offers both peace of mind and considerable profits.

MOUNT VICISSITUDES

The phrase *Margin of Safety* was coined by the late financial scholar Benjamin Graham (1894–1976), mentor to Warren Buffett and a generation of successful value investors. At age twenty, Graham, a wide-ranging intellectual, was offered positions on three separate Columbia University faculties: Greek and Latin philosophy, English, and mathematics. In addition to academia, he found a career on Wall Street. In 1934, he coauthored *Security Analysis,* the first serious tome about systematic investing in the stock market. Graham used *Margin of Safety* in a technical way to describe the attraction that a stock offered investors when it traded below what he termed its "intrinsic value." Both *Security Analysis* and a more accessible book, *The Intelligent Investor,* published in 1949, were enormously influential—perhaps too influential. After the run-up in the stock market in the 1950s (the best decade on record for large-cap equities), it became difficult, if not impossible, to find the sorts of companies that met Graham's criteria. But the epigraph from Virgil that Graham the classicist chose for *The Intelligent Investor* provides wisdom for the ages: "Through chances various, through all vicissitudes, we make our way." Today, the vicissitudes have mounted, and chance has been particularly cruel.

Graham believed so fervently in finding deeply discounted stocks that he wrote: "Confronted with a . . . challenge to distill the secret of sound investment into three words, we venture the following motto, Margin of Safety." He advocated buying stocks that were supercheap—for instance, stocks whose market capitalization (that is, the number of shares multiplied by the current stock price) was less than a company's cash and other liquid assets minus its debt. In other words, he wanted investors to buy dollar bills for 60 cents.

Later in this book, I will show you how to find Ben Graham–style deep-value stocks. But when I use the term *Margin of Safety* here, I mean to do more than simply identify companies that appear to be cheap. Pure value investing may have made sense in Graham's time, but life is no longer so simple.

You might say I am using Margin of Safety in an engineering sense. Instead of building levees to withstand a Category 3 hurricane, an engineer following a Margin of Safety strategy would build the dikes to withstand a Category 5 hurricane—even though such a storm appears less likely and the higher levees are definitely more costly. My strong belief is that Category 5 financial hurricanes will be far more frequent in the years to come. If you don't build a portfolio to withstand them, then, like residents of the Lower Ninth Ward of New Orleans, you will find your assets washed away, and rebuilding could take decades. What's surprising is how little it costs to raise Category 3 investing dikes to Category 5 status.

SOLID GAIN, MODEST PAIN

The Margin of Safety is something that practically every investor today craves but few know how to achieve. It is based on a trade-off: giving up a few percentage points on the upside for more protection on the downside. The bargain combines the likely chance of solid gain with the modest risk of pain.

Claims of strategies that can produce high gains with low pain are fantasy. The chance for high gain always risks high pain. If you want a real insurance policy against devastation, you need to pay the "premiums"—which come in the form of reduced profits. The premiums, in this case, however, can be quite low. For instance, over the past eighty-five years, a portfolio composed only of U.S. large-cap stocks returned an annual average of about 10 percent. If you had held a typical Margin of Safety portfolio over this period, your returns would have been about 8 percent. However, for the future, I believe that a conventional all-stock portfolio will expose the average investor to enormous risk and the near-certainty of some terribly painful stretches. I also doubt that, on average, such a portfolio will return as much as it did in the past. In such conditions, the Margin of Safety portfolio, with its effective insurance premium, makes for a smoother, less stressful ride. For example, in 2008, a portfolio with 90 percent allocated to stocks and 10 percent to bonds lost about one-third of its value, but a Margin of Safety portfolio—of the sort I advocate in this book—lost less than one-tenth.

"Solid gain, modest pain" seems both logical and desirable, but the Old Rulebook ignores this concept. Instead, the experts urged investors to build a stock portfolio that loses significant value in bear markets, with the expectation that the losses will be recouped (and then some) later.

As Graham himself wrote in 1949: "The investor may as well resign himself in advance to the probability, rather than the mere possibility, that most of his holdings will . . . decline the equivalent of one-third or more from their high point at various periods in the next five years."

And he was talking not just about the five years ahead but about *any* five-year period.

My Margin of Safety strategy is different from Graham's. It protects you against Category 5 hurricanes of the financial kind and does not require being "resigned" to losing "one-third or more" of your portfolio in a bad storm.

Sure, history shows that markets recover and stocks have been the best place to put your money over the long term. But this is of little solace, financial pundits notwithstanding. The older you get, the less long term is left for a recovery. Those close to retirement and dependent on drawing on assets can't take the chance that stock holdings will suddenly lose more than half their value, as the Standard & Poor's 500 Index did between June 2008 and March 2009. Even for younger investors, losing so much money in such a short time was horrifying. I'm sympathetic with those who say they don't ever want to go through the experience again. The message of this book is that you don't have to.

Severe losses affect the behavior of all investors, regardless of whether they are older and rich or younger and just starting to build a portfolio. When the value of your stocks drops sharply, you have a tendency to sell—often at just the wrong time. And, by the time you get back into the market, stocks typically have already made a sharp move upward. Financial advisors and historians can do all the preaching they want about the rewards of buying and holding stocks, but the truth is that many investors won't hang on during the bad times. My mission in this book is to address such real-life behavior head-on by laying out an approach that fits the new psychology of investors who have, with excellent reason, become gun-shy.

While bear markets can't be avoided, the losses you suffer can be modulated, to a significant degree. Think of a sine wave, with high highs and low lows.

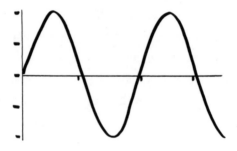

Now, smooth it out:

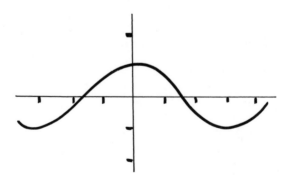

That is what Margin of Safety investing does. It makes the ride more comfortable. And it assures you that, if the market does take a dip, your investments will not be way down when it is time for you to retire.

A PREVIEW OF THE STRATEGY

As a preview, let me give you some specifics on the Margin of Safety strategy:

1. Reduce the proportion of stocks in your portfolio.
   - This is the single most dramatic change. It is necessary, and urgent. Like many financial advisors, I believed that if you were in your thirties or forties and planned to retire in your sixties or seventies, you could put all—or nearly all—of your retirement money into U.S. stocks. No longer.

2. For those stocks that you do own, make sure:
   - That you diversify internationally. It is imperative to own a significant chunk of shares of companies based in what have been known as emerging markets, but which I prefer to call *aspiring* markets (to emphasize the intensity of the desire of their people to prosper), especially those that represent the economy of the future, countries like Brazil, China, and India.

- That you own low-priced stocks in industries of the future, such as for-profit education, technology, and energy.

- That you own stocks, such as Procter & Gamble, that pay consistent dividends.

3. Make a substantial investment in bonds, especially:
   - U.S. Treasury bonds, called TIPS, that protect you against sharp increases in inflation.

   - Corporate bonds, even if they aren't given high ratings for safety.

4. Be sure you hedge, by which I mean . . .
   - Buy a bear fund, whose value rises when stock prices fall.

   - Consider derivatives (yes, derivatives!) that, in effect, put a collar on stock prices (limiting your upside in return for limiting your losses).

   - Expose yourself to currencies other than the dollar, even currencies of smaller, aspiring nations.

PARADIGM LOST

Today, building levees to withstand a Category 5 storm is not just an academic exercise. Such storms will be more frequent—because our financial climate has changed.

In fact, the *world* is changing. The U.S. stock market's performance in the first decade of the twenty-first century was no fluke. It reflected, to a large degree, a new global economic paradigm, which requires a new investing paradigm—a completely different approach from the one that was so successful in the past but is now outdated.

Here are four new realities that profoundly affect investing:

1. *The risks of financial catastrophe have grown exponentially with the development of larger and more complex investments, moving at faster speeds around the world.* The risks of other catastrophes, including terrorism on the scale of 9/11 or worse, and environmental disasters on the scale of the BP oil rig blowout or worse, have also increased.

2. *The United States is no longer the center of the economic universe.* Aspiring nations are driving the global economy, growing, in a normal year, about four times as fast as mature nations.

3. *Demographic imbalance (too low a ratio of youth to seniors) is weighing heavily on mature economies.* For example, when Social Security was started, forty-two workers supported every retiree. Today, the ratio is just three workers per retiree, and it's headed even lower.

4. *The financial crisis of 2008–2009 brought emergency measures—including vastly greater debt and nationalization of key businesses—that will depress growth in the United States, Europe, and Japan for years to come.*

Later chapters will expand on these changes, but let me offer more detail on the second one and its effect on investment strategy. Since so many large U.S. companies do business globally, financial pundits have argued that investors could buy American stocks—companies they know—and partake in international growth. This notion was reinforced by statistics showing that world markets had become more closely linked, moving up and down in tandem.

But favoring U.S. companies over those based in developing markets has proved to be a significant error. For the ten years ending December 8, 2010, the China Fund, a closed-end investment fund that's a good proxy for the Chinese market, returned an annual average of 27 percent while the Spiders exchange-traded fund, comprising the S&P 500 stocks (many of them with significant sales abroad), a proxy for the U.S. market, gained a yearly average of 1 percent. If you'd put $10,000 into the China Fund in December 2000, you would have had about $110,000 ten years later. If you'd put $10,000 into the U.S. equivalent, you would have $10,100. (By the way, both closed-end and exchange-traded funds, or ETFs, are portfolios of securities—stocks or bonds—that trade on major exchanges as if they were individual shares of stock.)

If we judge by market capitalization—that is, the product of the number of shares a company has issued multiplied by their current price—then the Industrial and Commercial Bank of China (ICBC), with 400,000 employees and 3.6 million corporate clients, is the largest bank in the world. China Life, by the same measurement, is the world's largest life insurance company. China Mobile is the largest telecom firm—more than twice the size of Verizon.

The good news is that it has become much easier for Americans to invest in such companies, and the political and corporate-governance obstacles to confidence are fading—though still not gone. (Both China Life and China Mobile trade on the New York Stock Exchange as American Depositary Receipts, or ADRs, so U.S. investors can buy and sell them as if they were domestic stocks. ICBC trades simultaneously on the Shanghai and Hong Kong exchanges, which are accessible to U.S. brokers. When it sold shares to the public in 2006, ICBC became the world's largest initial public offering.)

Investors who think they can ignore the stocks of nations like China (stocks in India and Brazil, by the way, have performed nearly as well as China's over recent years) are making an enormous mistake. Yes, U.S. companies sell *into* China, but Chinese companies—like China Mobile and China Life—utterly dominate the domestic-consumer market, which continues to boom, even while recession has slowed the rest of the world. The Chinese now buy more cars and trucks than Americans, and the vast majority of those vehicles are Chinese brands. Only 10 percent of Chinese buyers take out loans for their cars, compared with 80 percent of Americans. Imagine what will happen when consumer financing becomes even more widespread.

Of course, it's not hard to forget how the United States was written off in the 1980s by starry-eyed Japanophiles. America is not finished this time, either. The United States will continue to exercise its comparative advantage in technology, entrepreneurship, and management for decades to come. But a Margin of Safety strategy protects against the hubristic notion that America is the be-all and end-all, and American stocks—or other dollar-dominated assets—are the only securities that an American investor needs.

NOWHERE TO HIDE

My concerns about the future extend well beyond America's relative decline. I worry most of all about the enormous obligations with which this generation has saddled the next, and the next, and the next.

A few years ago, I posed a question at a Washington conference of the world's smartest fiscal economists. We had just finished a day talking about the unfunded Social Security and Medicare liabilities that had been built up over the past few decades. Promises to American retirees were valued—as I recall—at $50 trillion at that moment, in that day's dollars. (They are now over $100 trillion, or roughly $1 million per U.S. household.) President George W. Bush's attempt to reform Social Security and put it on a sounder footing had been killed by Congress, and no one wanted to tackle Medicare.

Yet, at the same time, with the economy perking along nicely, interest rates on thirty-year U.S. Treasury bonds were less than 5 percent, at a time when inflation was 3 percent. In other words, investors were not demanding much in return for lending their money to a government that would have an extremely difficult time meeting its obligations to seniors over the next thirty years and might decide to inflate its way out of the predicament. If investors were truly worried about a Social Security shortfall, you would think that interest rates—and inflation expectations—would be much higher.

So, I asked, "How do you guys reconcile low long-term interest rates with this Social Security and Medicare mess that no one wants to resolve?"

The answer from one of the economists was chilling: "The market believes the problem will be solved before the system collapses—though we can't tell you how." The other economists nodded.

That conversation took place well before the financial

crisis of 2008, when, to save the economy, the president and Congress added $2 trillion in debt in a year. Total deficits between 2011 and 2020 are estimated at $6 trillion, greater than the accumulated deficits of all previous years of American history—and, as we know, such guesses are often too low. Borrowing has consequences, and investors will feel them.

So why not just opt out? You can't. Investing is a game you have to play. You can't be a benchwarmer. You can't put money under the mattress. It's not a valid choice. In fact, it is a sure way to lose your purchasing power as inflation devours the currency. But hasn't inflation been low lately? Consumer Price Index increases averaged 2.9 percent in the 1990s and 2.5 percent in the first decade of the 2000s. Those figures are a bit below the overall average of 3 percent since 1926. But they are still damaging over the long term. Even at 2.5 percent inflation, the purchasing power of a dollar drops by about one-third in just fifteen years.

But if opting out is not an option, neither are the old strategies for investing, which once seemed tried and true. There is, however, an answer, and the chapters that follow will provide it.

BUILDING A HEDGE

Think of a Margin of Safety as a hedge, a backstop, a safety net. Everyone needs a hedge because we're all betting almost everything we have on black, and it's possible that red will come up.

Our jobs, the value of our houses, our ability to repay debt, our retirement savings, our health care—for all of these, we take the position of being "long" on the U.S. economy and long on its denominator of wealth, the dollar. In other words, we prosper when the economy grows briskly, when Gross Domestic Product rises and unemployment falls. The opposite of *long* is *short,* and, with financial investments, by going short, you can benefit from negative economic developments. When you short a stock, you borrow shares and immediately sell them, hoping to buy them back at a lower price, return the shares to the lender, and pocket the difference. You're cheering for a decline.

It's impossible to short your job (that is, win when you lose it) and impractical to short your house (which would mean selling it, moving into a rental, and buying it back when home prices fall) or your stamp collection or your Picasso lithographs.

But you can order your financial life so that you can gain—or at least not lose so much—when markets fall. One way is to use some of your money to short the market as a whole. You can, for instance, devote part of your portfolio to a special kind of fund that rises in value when stock prices fall. ProShares Short S&P 500, for example, uses derivatives—complicated financial instruments—to produce a return that is roughly the inverse of the popular index for large-capitalization stocks. If the index drops 30 percent, the fund will rise about 30 percent (actually, a bit less because of expenses). Later, we will explore funds and other investments that offer a short-side hedge.

But, for most investors, the best hedging strategy comes through allocation—that is, the way you divide up the assets (primarily stocks and bonds) that you own. Asset allocation is the most powerful investing tool you have. Allocation, rather than, for instance, your choice of particular stocks, is the most important determinant of your financial performance.

Later on, I will go into more detail about how to apportion your assets to meet your circumstances: your age, savings, needs, and tolerance of risk. But, for now, here is what the Margin of Safety strategy prescribes: a shift for nearly all investors to more bonds, less stocks.

FROM 80/20 TO 50/50

For example, if you previously believed that your $100,000 in financial assets should be allocated $80,000 to stocks and $20,000 to bonds, the Margin of Safety strategy advocates a shift from 80/20 to 50/50. And within your stock allocation, instead of owning only U.S. shares, you should own stocks of companies based in China, India, and other aspiring nations. Let's keep things simple to illustrate.

Morningstar, the research firm, maintains an excellent database of stock and bond returns, developed by economist Roger Ibbotson and starting in 1926. The statistics show that, through 2009, large-company U.S. stocks (represented by the S&P 500) returned an average of 9.8 percent annually; intermediate-term U.S. Treasury bonds, 5.3 percent.

Taking into account brokerage or mutual fund fees, let's assume that stocks return roughly 9 percent a year in the future and bonds return 5 percent. If we judge from more than eighty years of history, a $100,000 portfolio that is 90 percent stocks and 10 percent bonds will return about $8,600, or 8.6 percent annually.

Let's shift the allocation to 50/50. The returns drop to $7,000, or 7 percent annually—a decline of about 1½ percentage points a year. But the Morningstar/Ibbotson data show that a 50/50 allocation dramatically reduces volatility—the risk that you will lose a lot of money in a relatively short time. The biggest one-year loss since 1926 for a 90 percent stock/10 percent bond portfolio was 40 percent, but with a 50/50 allocation, the worst one-year loss was 25 percent. The worst five-year performance, during the Great Depression, produced an average annual loss for the 90/10 portfolio of 10 percent. But with a 50/50 allocation, the worst five-year loss was 3 percent annualized. Over five years, an annual loss of 10 percent reduces the value of your $100,000 portfolio to $59,000, but a loss of 3 percent reduces it only to $86,000.

If history predicts the future, then your allocation hedge—your insurance policy—is costing you $1,600 a year per $100,000 invested, but it protects against a worst-case historic loss that reduces your nest egg by an extra $27,000. And, if the future is even worse than the past—which I believe it will be—then the insurance policy may be even more valuable.

My past recommendations for the bond part of your portfolio were exclusively federal securities with short- and medium-term maturities. I urged investors to stay away from corporate bonds because their returns were not much higher than those of Treasuries and because corporate bonds carried roughly the same risk as corporate stocks—but stocks returned more. But in the past ten years, the world of bonds has changed as well and, for reasons I will explain in a later chapter, I now advocate that corporate debt, which is what a bond represents, has a key role to play in your investment strategy.

Bonds that you intend to hold to maturity are subject to two kinds of risk: credit risk (the chance that you might not get paid back) and inflation risk (the chance that rising prices will mean that, when you do get paid back, the dollars you receive will purchase far less than the dollars you invested). Neither of these risks can be entirely eliminated, but I will show you how to mitigate them. For instance, to guard against inflation, you can buy TIPS, or Treasury Inflation-Protected Securities, whose return rises with the Consumer Price Index. Today, not just corporates, but even Treasuries, may involve credit risk, as the U.S. government takes on a growing debt burden. That risk is more difficult to hedge against, but I will show you how.

The strategy to pursue with bonds is the "5 Percent Solution"; that is, in times of low to normal inflation, you should shoot for average returns of 5 percent. While you are always able to get higher yields by taking on more risk or longer maturities, you should resist. Now is the time to give bonds the respect they deserve.

YOU'RE ON YOUR OWN

Not only did the events of 2008 and 2009 devastate the portfolios of investors, they also demonstrated that you're on your own. You can't count on the government to bail you out (not unless you're General Motors or Citigroup). You can't count on your banker or broker. Or your mutual fund manager. Or your employer, for that matter.

Politicians talk about toughening financial rules and getting more inspectors out into the field, but you really can't rely on the regulators or their regulations, as the Ponzi scheme perpetrated by Bernard Madoff dramatically showed. Arthur Levitt, the longest-serving chairman in the history of the Securities and Exchange Commission, puts it bluntly, "A very skillful criminal can almost always outfox the regulator or the overseer." Even worse, when investors rely on regulators, they let their own guard down and are more likely to make mistakes.

Self-reliance sounds like a frightening prospect, but many of the old rules of investing still apply, and they are not difficult to follow. Here are some of the eternal verities:

- **Diversify.** Many individuals and foundations put every dollar of their financial assets into Madoff's fictional investment pool. Of course, I sympathize with these people, but what they did was just plain stupid. As employees of Enron learned in 2001, the value of an investment can sometimes go to zero. There is only one sure way to cushion the effect of such an event: Spread your money around. Some of the biggest names in global business suffered terrible declines in the last decade: AIG, General Motors, Citigroup. Even General Electric, once the most admired company in the world, dropped from $42 a share to $7 in the space of six months. And look what happened to Iceland! Let's be clear: No one can predict such calamities. But if you diversify, you don't have to be in the prediction business. Diversification occurs not just within the stock category but across asset classes. You need bonds as well as stocks, and you need to invest in cash and securities denominated in currencies other than the U.S. dollar.

- **Show me the money.** The best Margin of Safety is cash in the pocket, and providing that cash is a major objective of the New Rulebook. I advocate solid, dividend-paying stocks—even if they aren't in the sexiest industries. One good example is a financially sound and consistently profitable global consumer-products firm, like Procter & Gamble. In December 2010, it had a yield of 3.1 percent—that is, its annual dividend payout was 3.1 percent of its stock price at the time. In the second half of the twentieth century, it was rare for a blue-chip stock to yield nearly as much as a ten-year U.S. Treasury bond, but in December 2010, such a bond was paying interest of only 3.2 percent. Enterprise Products Partners, a natural gas firm, is set up as a limited partnership rather than a corporation, but its units trade like any other stock on the New York Stock Exchange and had a yield in October 2010 of 5.7 percent. Many energy limited partnerships pay dividends that bounce up and down over the years, but Enterprise has been steady, its payout rising every quarter since 1999. Research shows that stocks that pay dividends are more stable in their prices than nondividend payers. Dividends also are the best indicator of the health of a business. For one thing, you can't fake cash. For another, managers are reluctant to cut their dividends, so they try hard to keep them at sustainable levels; as a result, payouts are a good predictor of future growth.

- **Markets are efficient.** In tough times, especially, investors feel pressure to time the market—to buy and sell stocks in anticipation of near-term price moves. This approach, called *market timing,* simply does not work, not even in the new world of post-2008 investing. John Bogle, the founder of Vanguard mutual funds, put it best: "After nearly fifty years in this business, I do not know of anybody who has done it successfully and consistently. I do not know anybody who knows anybody who has done it successfully and consistently." Markets are, in general, efficient. Today's price absorbs everything that can be known about a company today, including the consensus on the course of its business tomorrow. So today's price is right, and, unless you have illegal insider information, you can't divine tomorrow's price. You can certainly make long-term predictions about the success of a business or an industry, and buy stocks accordingly. But timing the market remains a fool's errand.

The Margin of Safety strategy encompasses these truths—and more—from the Old Rulebook and adds new ones. Chapter 5 lays out all rules in summary form.

A BOLT FROM THE BLUE

My goal is to protect you against calamitous financial events, which, remarkably enough, were rarely taken into account by financial economists in the past. Their concern was volatility—the extremes of the ups and downs of prices. Think of a roller coaster that starts at sea level. It might rise 100 feet, plunge 50 feet, rise another 30, fall 60, and so on. In the end, it comes back to where it started. You can calculate the volatility—that is, the steepness and frequency of the ups and downs—and this metric is important to know, especially if you're averse to stomach-churning rides. But volatility isn't the only risk on a roller coaster. It could be struck by lightning, or a car could go off the tracks. The chance of such calamities is more important to know about than volatility, but it is also harder—or even impossible—to calculate.

In terms of traditional risk, or volatility, an investment isn't risky at all if it returns precisely the same—say, 5 percent after inflation—year after year. It has no ups and downs, like a roller coaster that travels on level rails. By looking at history, we can quantify the risks of stocks and conclude, for example, that, if you hold a diversified portfolio for five years, your chances of losing money are just one in ten. But there is another kind of risk, akin to the chance of a roller coaster flying off the tracks.

In the 1920s, an economist named Frank Knight drew

a distinction between risks we can count (and count *on*)—gleaned through data points of history and associated with volatility—and what he called "a higher form of uncertainty not susceptible to measurement and hence to elimination." Knight has largely been forgotten, but it appears he got it right.

Knightian uncertainty is a bolt from the blue, the toppling of the World Trade Center's twin towers, the severe economic contraction produced throughout Europe in the 1720s after the collapse of John Law's Mississippi Scheme,* or the five-month shutdown of the London Stock Exchange after World War I broke out.

The shock of the last decade falls into the Knightian category: a crisis that sent home prices tumbling for the first time in half a century, robbed stocks of half their value, and pushed major businesses into bankruptcy. If you're a typical investor, it is the risk of such a calamity that worries you most. In return for some calamity insurance, you should be willing to lower your ambitions.

But you don't have to lower them much. At a cost of 1 or 2 percentage points a year, you can invest with a real safety net to catch you if you fall. If that sounds like a good deal to you, now is the time to begin.

---

* The story of John Law, a Scottish financier who founded a French trading company that sold vast amounts of shares and bonds to the public, and then disintegrated, is recounted in Charles Mackay's essential book, *Extraordinary Delusions and the Madness of Crowds*, published in 1841. Charles Kindleberger's *Manias, Panics, and Crashes* (1978) is an update of Mackay and also frighteningly edifying.

1

THE WORLD IS CHANGING

The premise of this book is that investors need a new strategy to adapt to a new world. But before we get to the strategy itself, we need to understand how the world has changed. The changes fall into two categories: first, the relationship of the United States to the rest of the world, and, second, the acceleration of risk itself. Let's begin with some history . . .

The most impressive chart in all of investing is repro-duced annually in the *Ibbotson Stocks, Bonds, Bills, and Inflation Classic Yearbook,* published by Morningstar. It shows the growth of a single dollar placed in a portfolio of U.S. large-capitalization stocks, starting at the end of 1925, with dividends plowed back into the same shares. At the left side of the chart, there's a squiggle that quickly falls (the Crash of 1929 and the Great Depression), then starts rising steeply, almost without letup, at a forty-five-degree angle. By the end of 2007, the solitary dollar had become $3,253.

For eighty-two years, the S&P 500 rose an average of a

little more than 10 percent annually. Through the power of compounding, an investment returning 10 percent doubles roughly every seven years and rises by a factor of sixteen every generation.

Of course, the drama of such charts is typically determined by where you start, but, in the case of the U.S. stock market, it really does not matter so much. Research by Jeremy Siegel of the Wharton School of Business on U.S. stocks going back to 1802 has shown similar results.

Even after taking inflation into account, stocks have returned an average of about 7 percent annually—again, going back to the nineteenth century. At that rate, the purchasing power of an investment doubles every ten years, quadruples every twenty, and increases sixteenfold every forty years.

It's not hard to understand why U.S. stocks have been such popular investments. Their rising prices have been no fluke. Share values reflect—though not on a perfect, year-to-year basis—the growth of the world's greatest economy. With Gross Domestic Product (the sum of all the goods and services we produce) increasing at between 6 and 7 percent—its average for the latter half of the twentieth century, with inflation included—there was good reason to believe that stocks would continue to rise, as they had in the past.

In fact, a major problem for economists who looked at U.S. stocks was not why they had risen so much but why they had not risen *more*—especially given the consistency of the stock market's performance. Stocks beat bonds by about five percentage points a year, and the two assets had risk profiles over long periods that were surprisingly similar. This was a conundrum—the "equity premium puzzle," as economists called it.

To be exact, a portfolio of the 500 largest large-cap stocks showed gains in sixty-eight out of seventy-eight overlapping five-year periods between 1926 and 2007 (that is, from the start of 1926 to the start of 1931, 1927–1932, etc.). For ten-year periods, the record of gains was close to perfect: seventy-one out of seventy-three.* For long-term U.S. Treasury bonds, risk measured this way was almost the same. What gives?

In the 1990s, it appeared that investors, who were perhaps irrationally fearful in the past, started getting wise to this attractive risk-and-return picture for stocks compared with bonds and were, quite reasonably, buying up stocks and, thus, bidding up stock prices. Starting in early 2000 with the collapse of tech stocks, this process of shucking off risk aversion stopped abruptly. The decade that followed was, as noted in the Introduction, the worst in stock market history, as recorded by Ibbotson. The era of the Great Depression (1929–1940) doesn't come close. The ten-year period that ended in February 2009 produced an average annual stock market loss of 5.8 percent after infla-

---

* The Ibbotson/Morningstar yearbook I cited on page 29 is the source for these historic data. It is well worth purchasing: http://corporate.morningstar.com/ ib/asp/subject.aspx?xmlfile=1414.xml.

tion. This means that a $100,000 investment in early 1999 would have buying power of about $55,000 by early 2009.

So, judging from this devastation, what conclusion should we draw?

TIME TO ARGUE WITH HISTORY

Of course, *some* ten-year period has to finish last, and many people believe that 1999–2009 is an outlier, a weird occurrence, a blip. When we look at the vast sweep of the past, why worry about the aberrations? If you can put your money to work for twenty years or more—as anyone under age forty-five who plans to retire at sixty-five can do—history shows that stocks recover and produce handsome profits for the patient investor.

Yes, but while history is often a good indicator of the future, it is hardly a perfect predictor. At the start of 2001, if you judge strictly from history, no African-American would ever get elected president of the United States, the New Orleans Saints would never win the Super Bowl, and 3,000 civilians would never be killed by America's foreign adversaries on a single day. Sometimes, the game changes.

My conclusion with regard to stocks is that similar game-changing forces are in play. It's time to argue with history. A pure buy-and-hold, stock-focused strategy— one that the past seems to assure and one that I urged on my readers for many years—no longer has validity. The reason is not that the first decade of the twenty-first century was so miserable for stocks. The reason is that the world is changing—in dramatic ways. Every investor must take those changes into account, or face the consequences.

Notice I say *is changing*—not *has changed*. The price of a share of stock is typically defined as the present value (that is, the value in today's dollars) of all the cash that the share is expected to throw off in dividends during the life of the underlying company. We don't have to get too technical here. Just understand that stock prices are determined by *expectations*—by what people today think will happen in the future.

While some of the dramatic changes have already occurred, the most dramatic are still in process. The future is ultimately unknowable, as the quote from Peter L. Bernstein at the start of this book reminds us, but the likely course of the changes is becoming more and more clear.

TOO MUCH MATURITY

There are strong indications that the United States and other developed economies have reached maturity. While the United States has grown at an average annual rate of about 3.5 percent, after inflation, since World War II, the country now appears on track to join Europe and Japan at growth of half or two-thirds of that historic pace. The Congressional Budget Office, in fact, is predicting that the

U.S. economy will grow at an average rate of just 2.3 percent from 2016 to 2020.* Those figures, in my view, might be too optimistic. The shorthand for GDP growth is the increase in workers plus the increase in productivity (that is, what each worker produces). Boosting the number of Americans at work by even 0.5 percent annually is going to be difficult. Add to that a productivity rise of 1.5 percent, and you're at 2 percent, but productivity could just as easily rise at 1 percent, or even less.

While these numbers seem tiny, a single percentage point can matter a lot. For instance, if population growth is 1 percent annually, then a 3 percent GDP growth rate after inflation produces a per-capita increase in GDP of 2 percent. At that rate, real incomes (and thus purchasing power) double in about a generation. But if GDP per-capita growth is only 0.6 percent, it will take well over a century for real incomes to double.

The U.S. economy is not coming to a screeching halt, but the dimming prospects for a briskly rising standard of living should worry every investor. My view several years ago was that "It's *not* the economy, stupid," that investors have enough to worry about. You should be in stocks for many, many years, and, "over the long term, the Fed and the [U.S.] economy behave with remarkable consistency." They have in the past, but I now have serious doubts that

---

* You can find the August 2010 CBO report on the budget and the economy, chock full of important statistics and projections, here: http://www.cbo.gov/ ftpdocs/117xx/doc11705/08-18-Update.pdf.

this consistency (*and* levels of growth) will carry into the future.

Why? Three reasons. The first is demographic. The United States and other mature economies have an expensive, stultifying imbalance between young and old in their societies—the result of these factors:

- *Dramatically lower fertility rates.* The number of births per American woman has dropped from 3.7 in 1960 to 2.1 today.

- *Longer life spans.* Between 1929 and 1931, just before Social Security was enacted, the average American lived to be just fifty-nine; today, seventy-eight.

- *Earlier retirements.* In 1950, three-quarters of males were working between ages sixty-two and sixty-four; by 1997, the proportion had fallen to fewer than half.

So, here are the consequences: In 1945, the ratio of workers to retirees in the United States was 40:1; by 1950, it had dropped to 16:1; by 1960, to 5:1. Today, a little more than three workers support each retiree; by the 2030s, the ratio will be just two workers to one.

The second reason mature economies are slowing is harder to explain. Call it decadence. Begin with the fact that economic growth is a relatively new phenomenon. Through the work of Angus Maddison and other economic historians, we know that before the early nine-teenth century, there was essentially no global economic growth—an increase in real GDP of about 0.1 percent a year. The industrial revolution dramatically changed the picture, and from 1820 to 1998, growth in developed nations, per capita, averaged 1.7 percent annually; in developing nations, a little less than 1 percent annually.

But will incomes—especially in developed countries, where the bulk of the historic growth has occurred already—continue to soar? In 1931, John Maynard Keynes, in an essay titled "Economic Possiblities for Our Grandchildren," looked at these growth patterns and predicted that, within 100 years, the "economic problem"—the struggle to rise above subsistence and earn enough to enjoy a good life—would be solved, with standards of living rising to four to eight times their 1930 levels.

Keynes was impressively prescient—up to a point. In fact, for sixty or seventy years, standards of living rose at the pace he predicted, but then—in mature economies—rates leveled off. What Keynes and other optimists did not count on was this: People begin to decide that they are happy with what they have and choose comfort and risk aversion—based on the protections of a burgeoning central government—over growth. That has been the case in Europe. The United States now has a per-capita GDP 40 percent greater than that of France—for the simple reason that Americans work much more. Americans work longer hours, take fewer vacations, and retire later. The

French, Italians, and Germans, in their prosperity, have chosen leisure and swaddling by the state. This appears to be where the United States is headed as well.

The propensity of governments to overspend and overtax and to make poor judgments about social programs and regulations is nothing new, but in resilient market economies, human ingenuity and persistence have overcome bad governance. In 1849, Thomas Macaulay wrote in his *History of England* that "the constant progress of physical knowledge and the constant effort of every man to better himself" are such powerful forces that they can surmount "ordinary misfortune" and "ordinary misgovernment." He went on: "It has often been found that profuse expenditure, heavy taxation, absurd commercial restriction, corrupt tribunals, disastrous wars, seditions, persecutions, conflagrations, inundations, have not been able to destroy capital so fast as the exertions of private citizens have been able to create it."

This is a lovely sentiment with which I don't disagree. But pay special attention to the adjective *ordinary* modifying *misfortune* and *misgovernment*. Governments (and nongovernment actors, ranging from terrorists to businesses) now wield the power, thanks in large part to technology, to make decisions that produce misfortune that goes well beyond the "ordinary."

The third and final reason for slowing growth in developed nations is the response to the recession of 2008–2009 and the sluggishness that followed. In a panic over the political and social consequences of a downturn, governments, now blessed with more levers to influence consumer and business behavior, spent far beyond their incomes and took on huge amounts of debt—the U.S. annual deficit in 2010, for instance, exceeded one-tenth of GDP—in order to flood their economies with cash and stimulate a recovery.

Whether this strategy was smart can be debated, but there is no escaping the costs. Over the next ten years and more, these governments will be faced with large bills for their borrowing—bills that must be paid with money that would otherwise have been used for private-sector investment.

In fiscal year 2008, the deficit was $160 billion, or about $1,500 for every American household. In 2009, it was nearly ten times that figure. Even in the rosiest Congressional Budget Office scenario, the deficit will continue at about a half-trillion a year. The global financial crisis was caused by debt, and its short-term solution was debt. Both the federal government and U.S. consumers are now saddled with enormous amounts of debt. Think of it as a load you carry on your shoulders. It's harder to move forward with such a burden.

In their book *This Time Is Different*, economists Carmen Reinhart of the University of Maryland and Ken Rogoff of Princeton looked at eight centuries of financial crises and found that they produce a legacy of debt. After such a crisis, government debt, on average, doubles in three years (for the United States, that's about right: from $5.9 trillion at the start of fiscal 2009 to a projected $10 trillion three years later). And, then, there's a legacy of unemployment—a jump, on average, of seven percentage points (it's been six in the United States) and a five-year period of lowered employment levels. For us, it could be even longer.

My own forecast is that we will see slow growth in the United States, Europe, and Japan—on the order of 2 percent—for the next decade and that this slow growth will affect the price of stocks negatively. I could be wrong—no one can tell the future with consistency and accuracy—but I am worried enough to urge investors to protect themselves by shifting to the Margin of Safety strategy and establishing a low-cost safety net to cushion any fall. If the economy booms, it's hardly a tragedy. You will still achieve excellent returns with this strategy, and your salary and the value of your home will be rising as well.

CHINA 44, USA 27

As a result of these three forces—demographics, decadence, and debt—the United States and other developed nations will no longer be the epicenter of the economic and financial universe. The economies of developed (mature) nations are losing steam and those of developing (aspiring) nations are gaining. This is not necessarily a reason for despair. You can, after all, invest in aspiring markets—but, again, you need protection because aspiring markets won't match the relative stability that mature markets have displayed (well, until recently) for the past half-century and more.

Developed countries today account for a slight majority of global GDP, but they will soon be overtaken by developing countries, which are growing six percentage points faster each year. Simple question: In which business would you rather be a shareholder—one that's growing at 8 percent or one that's growing at 2 percent?

This is a profound change. The historical data show that during the nineteenth and twentieth centuries, developed nations grew far faster than developing nations. But, in the spring of 2009, when the Pew Research Center asked Americans to name the world's leading economic power, 44 percent said China and 27 percent the United States.

In terms of actual output, the U.S. economy is between two and three times the size of China (depending on whether you compute China's GDP at purchasing-power parity—that is, by what China's currency actually buys— or at the exchange rate between the countries; either method has its merits). On a per-capita basis, U.S. GDP is six to ten times greater than Chinese. The respondents clearly got the facts wrong, but the sentiment that China is growing far faster than the United States and will soon become the dominant global economic power is correct. And stocks, remember, are priced by such perceptions.

But so what if developing countries are outstripping

developed nations? Economics is not a zero-sum game. In other words, Chinese economic gains don't produce American losses. As I write, China's GDP is projected to grow 10.2 percent during 2010 while U.S. GDP growth is forecast at 2.6 percent. If China's growth were just 2 percent, would the United States have been better off in 2010? Not at all. In fact, with Chinese demand lower, the U.S. economy would almost certainly have performed worse. Chinese exports to the United States drive down prices for consumers here, and, as the Chinese themselves grow richer, American companies can sell them goods they could not afford before.

The zero-sum competition model (we do worse if they do better) is inaccurate, but comparisons still count— especially for investors. What is remarkable about the last decade is that emerging markets, like China and Brazil, did so much better than developed markets, such as the United States. The difference is reflected in stock prices. While U.S. stocks were flat for the ten years ending in early December 2010, Vanguard's Emerging Markets Stock Index fund rose an average of 15 percent a year. I believe this is no accident but, rather, a harbinger of even greater disparities to come.

Aspiring markets stocks did well because the underlying economies of the companies where they were based did well. For most of the world, the recession ended in 2009, but developed economies still appeared anemic at the close of 2010. *The Economist* magazine's consensus of experts projected 2011 GDP growth in Germany at just 2 percent; France, 1.4; Japan, 1.3. The United States is expected to do better, but even 2.3 percent is no great shakes coming off a terrible decline (by contrast, GDP jumped more than 7 percent in 1984 after the bad recession of that era).

Now look at what's happening outside mature economies. Twenty of the twenty-one Asian, Mideast, and Latin American emerging economies that *The Economist* tracks have projected growth that will exceed that of the United States in 2011. The GDP increase is estimated at 8.9 percent for China; 8.6 percent for India; 5.9 percent for Chile; and 6 percent for Indonesia.

There are good reasons to believe that the growth of developing economies will remain robust for the next decade and beyond:

1. Unlike in the past, these economies have the capital—both homegrown and attracted from abroad—to start new businesses and build current ones. For the first nine months of 2009 alone, "new lending by Chinese banks has injected $1.3 trillion into the world economy," according to the *Washington Post*. Beneficiaries include even mature-economy firms, including Southwest Airlines and the Woolworths supermarket chain in Australia.

2. Governments in aspiring economies are promoting growth-oriented policies. India, for instance,

is simplifying its business tax system in what could be the "single most important initiative in the fiscal history" of the country, according to Satya Poddar of Ernst & Young and Ehtisham Admad of the London School of Economics.

3. And these countries have a more productive ratio of young workers to older retirees. For example, only 6 percent of Indonesians are over sixty-five years old, compared with 16 percent of the French and 22 percent of the Japanese.

SUPPLY AND DEMAND, BOTH

There are two sides to the attraction of aspiring economies: supply and demand. On the supply side, natural resources are plentiful, labor is cheaper than in mature markets, and, as education levels rise and more capital is invested there, workers are becoming more efficient. But change on the demand side is even more dramatic. With incomes growing, the citizens of aspiring economies are moving beyond the necessities. They're eating better food, buying their own homes, purchasing cars.

But, again, it's not just that the developing economies are doing better; the developed economies are doing worse. Demographics matter. In developed countries— especially Europe and Japan, but the United States as well—a larger and larger proportion of the population comprises old people. They do not participate in the workforce; instead, under the pay-as-you-go government pension systems of the United States and other countries, retirees absorb the earnings of younger workers. The costs of maintaining older people will only rise—from health care expenses alone—as they continue to live longer.

There are solutions to the demographic imbalance, but they involve political changes that are both difficult and, even if they could be accomplished, destabilizing. One answer is increased immigration—the movement of younger people, many of them Muslim, to developed nations from developing ones. That's already happening, but at not nearly the pace to provide enough young workers to support retirees. Another answer is a new attitude toward entitlements in nations with strong welfare states—a shift, for example, from the pay-as-you-go model for retirement benefits, with the young funding the old, to a savings model, with the old funding their own retirement from savings and insurance purchases they make when they are young.

A more likely answer, at least for the short term, is that developed nations will try to preserve their prosperity by selling off their assets to developing nations. That is already happening in the case of government bonds, but we can expect the process to accelerate with real estate, corporate bonds, and equities. Aspiring nations—many of which in a generation will have GDP per capita rivaling developed nations—will own the pick of the productive assets of those mature economies.

FLAT-OUT RISKIER

The second way that the world has changed is that it has become flat-out riskier. Let's look at the traditional measure of risk first: volatility. In a tightly connected global economy, where capital can rush quickly to hot new assets and away from suddenly dangerous old ones, large financial institutions are at greater risk of suffering severe disruptions or collapse, and they are more apt to suffer these disasters at the same time. (As a metaphor, think of a large crowd of passengers rushing from one side of a sailboat to the other.) Don't expect stronger regulations—such as higher capital requirements—to prevent meltdowns. After all, the nature of the banking business is to use leverage to profit from loans. To achieve leverage, a bank has to borrow on top of a small base of equity capital; otherwise, the business simply won't work. Increase capital requirements too much, and lending will dry up, something governments just won't tolerate.

The difference is that, in the past, bank failures were isolated or regional. Today, they are global. Among the biggest losers in the U.S. subprime debacle were Credit Agricole of France, CIBC of Canada, Mizuho Financial of Japan, and the Royal Bank of Scotland. It is swiftly moving information that stimulates the flow of capital and while, overall, that's a good thing (capital should go where it's best used), sometimes investors get it wrong—as they certainly did when they rushed into risky mortgages—and consequences can be grave.

As a believer in the power of markets to solve problems, I suspect that mechanisms will be discovered to dampen this dangerous volatility, but even here, the prospect isn't pretty. Short-term solutions would use financial engineering, through derivatives. But the history of derivatives is not encouraging. For example, commodities futures contracts were invented to give farmers stability. Unsure what the price of wheat will be at harvest time, a farmer, when he plants his crop, enters into a contract to sell the wheat at a fixed price in, say, six months. If the price of wheat rises substantially, the farmer won't get the extra profit, but, if the price of wheat falls, he's protected.

In real life, however, agricultural commodities markets have become giant betting pools for speculators who are wagering on the chances of drought in Nebraska or the demand for bread in Russia. Those speculators (call them investors, if you like) provide the liquidity—the ready cash—that makes markets function, but, since the speculators base their transactions on leverage, small price movements can have huge profit-and-loss effects, which themselves boost volatility.

Don't forget that the crisis in the mortgage markets was founded on derivatives that provided insurance. Investment houses bought protection for assets, like subprime mortgages, that they knew were risky. That would seem to be responsible behavior—except that the insurers themselves, including the world's largest insurance company, AIG, could not stand behind their obligations.

For the near future, it makes sense to assume that volatility is here to stay—and that you need to find ways to protect yourself against it.

FROM RISK TO CATASTROPHE

Investing, in its simplest terms, is an act of faith. You take money you have earned and, instead of using it for consumption right now, you put it somewhere you trust. Over the years, if you put it in the right place, your original stake will grow dramatically.

By relinquishing control, you assume risk. Suppose I invest $100,000 in a partnership to build an office building. The partnership raises a total of $10 million, so my share is 1 percent. The building takes three years to design and construct, then perhaps another year to lease. At the end of those four years, the partnership hopes to sell the property to a real estate management company for around $20 million. My share would become $200,000. Under this scenario, I double my money, for a compound annual return on my investment of 19 percent.

But over those four years, there might be all sorts of

unforeseen developments: a freak storm could devastate the building site, a change in zoning regulations could make it difficult to rent offices to high-paying tenants, interest rates might rise and loans associated with the project might become far more expensive, or the economy could take a nosedive, leaving the building nearly empty.

In fact, there are so many risks that, as an investor without special knowledge of real estate (or even *with* it), I can't possibly assess them all. I take solace in the fact that the project's managing partner has a good track record, but I understand that I could lose my entire stake. I weigh the possible risk and reward, and decide that the investment makes sense—or doesn't.

Now, let's consider investing in stock. The challenge is similar. Before you buy shares of General Electric, you might examine the balance sheet or read about the prospects for sales of giant turbines or sophisticated medical machines or lightbulbs. You consult experts and consider GE's reputation, but, in the end, you make a rough calculation of the company's likely risks and rewards, and make your decision.

As I noted earlier, diversification reduces overall risk, so if you buy a bundle of stocks—such as those of the 500 companies that comprise the S&P 500 Index, you reduce the dangers of putting all your eggs in one basket.

By examining the past, we can make guesses about the risks of bundles of stock in the future. The tool to use is standard deviation, which measures the way that points of data vary around their own average. If equities produced the same return day after day, then the stock market's standard deviation would be zero. But, of course, stock prices fluctuate a lot in the short term.

In a study, Donald G. Bennyhoff, a senior investment analyst for the Vanguard Group, pointed out that during the eighty years following 1926, the average standard deviation for U.S. stocks over each one-year period was about twenty percentage points. That means that in two-thirds of the years, returns will range roughly between a 30 percent gain and a 10 percent loss. Now, that's risky.

But over longer periods, the volatility of stocks falls dramatically. If you keep an S&P 500 portfolio for five years, the standard deviation is just 8.5 percent. If you hold stocks for twenty years, history shows that, two-thirds of the time, average annual returns will range between a high of 15 percent and a low of 8 percent. The highest average annual return for the sixty-five such periods since 1926 was 18 percent; the lowest, 3 percent. That's not very risky at all.

Many investors fail to grasp this historical pattern. They focus on the near-term volatility. And why not? It's right in front of their faces. "In large part," writes Benny-hoff, "it is this disconnect between the expected lower risk of an investment in stocks over the long run and the expected higher risk of such an investment in the short run that creates doubt and can foster poor decision-making under stress."

This disconnect is at the heart of the advice that most financial experts have given for decades: Don't be myopic about risk. Yes, it looks scary in the short term, but everything will turn out fine in the long term.

I used to give that advice myself, but no longer. One reason, as I noted in the Introduction, is human behavior. We can't expect people to be as rational as Bennyhoff wants them to be. In the face of a 42 percent drop in the value of the S&P 500 in just three months in the fall of 2008, investors became frightened to death. With such volatility, you can't build a rational strategy on the assumption that investors will courageously hang on. A second reason, as I said just now, is that the increased volatility we have seen lately is no aberration. It is the result of an interconnected global financial system.

But a *third* reason for doubting the advice to invest merely by staying the course with a stock portfolio is that the definition of risk used by financial experts is woefully incomplete. Or, to put it another way, when it comes to bad things that can happen to your portfolio, conventional risk doesn't come close to summing up all the dangers. There's another kind of risk—the risk that the roller coaster will fly off the tracks.

"WE SIMPLY DO NOT KNOW!"

This second kind of risk was first codified by the economist Frank Knight, who grew up in poverty on a farm in Illinois, the eldest of eleven children, and eventually taught at the University of Chicago for more than forty years, starting in 1929. He used the term *uncertainty* to describe this other kind of risk. Knight wrote in a largely impenetrable book titled *Risk, Uncertainty and Profit,* "Uncertainty must be taken in a sense radically distinct from the familiar notion of Risk, from which it has never been properly separated."

Conventional risk involves probability that we can clearly identify and measure. When you flip a coin, for instance, you know the odds are that half the time heads will come up and half the time tails. You can get a run of ten heads in a row, but on each new flip the odds are 50/50 that heads will appear, and over thousands of flips, heads and tails will each come up roughly the same number of times.

When financial analysts speak of stock market risk, they are talking about volatility—that is, the extremes of the market's ups and downs. This is roughly the same kind of quantifiable risk we see in coin flips. Measurements of volatility, such as standard deviation and beta (the variation of prices of individual stocks or bonds compared with what other securities in their class are doing) use history as a guide. For example, the S&P 500 Index has declined in twenty-four of the past eighty-four calendar years. Thus, in any one year, your chance of losing money in a broadly diversified portfolio is 29 percent.

This is the kind of risk most investors understand, if only intuitively. In his book, *Against the Gods*, a history of risk, economist Peter L. Bernstein wrote, "Extrapolation of past frequencies is the favored method for arriving at judgments about what lies ahead. . . . Experienced people come to recognize that inflation is somehow associated with high interest rates . . . and that driving at high speed along city streets is dangerous."

When he used the term *uncertainty*—which he also called *ambiguity* or plain old *ignorance*—Knight meant risk of the "unmeasurable" or "nonquantifiable" type.

In *The General Theory of Employment, Interest and Money*, published in 1937, Lord Keynes extended Knight's ideas about uncertainty, writing, "The sense in which I am using the term is that in which the prospect of a European war is uncertain, or the price of copper and the rate of interest 20 years hence, or the obsolescence of a new invention. . . . About these matters, there is no scientific basis on which to form any calculable probability whatever. We simply do not know!"

That's a good motto for every investor in this age of Knightian uncertainty—an age in which rogue nations like Iran and North Korea are on the way to developing nuclear weapons that can be delivered by long-range missiles (and, in North Korea's case, can already be delivered in seagoing containers or perhaps a suitcase), in which countries like China appear to have the computing power to shut down power grids on the other side of the earth or to erase your banking records. Of course, while nonquantifiable, the nuclear and cyberwarfare risks can be termed *known unknowns,* as former Defense Secretary Donald Rumsfeld was fond of saying. Even more scary are the *unknown unknowns,* also called *black swans.*

The investor Nassim Nicholas Taleb introduced the concept of black swans in his book *Fooled by Randomness,* paraphrasing the Scottish philosopher David Hume: "No amount of observations of white swans can allow the inference that all swans are white, but the observation of a single black swan is sufficient to refute that conclusion."

In other words, earthshaking surprises happen. The fact that something hasn't occurred in the past—such as a single-day decline of 23 percent in the Dow Jones Industrial Average (unknown prior to October 19, 1987)—doesn't mean it *can't* occur.

Here's an example of flawed reasoning of the sort that many investors practice—reduced by Taleb to a nice absurdity: "I have just completed a thorough statistical examination of the life of President Bush. For 58 years, close to 21,000 observations, he did not die once. I can hence pronounce him as immortal, with a high degree of statistical significance." You may conclude that just because a company has increased its profits every year since inception, it will keep doing so. Don't believe it.

Consider liquidity—that is, the condition of easy sales and purchases of investments. It's something we take for granted, at least as far as most stocks and bonds are concerned. But the Harvard historian Niall Ferguson reminds us that less than a century ago, liquidity quickly dried up on the world's key exchanges:

Buoyant financial markets had initially shrugged off the assassination of Archduke Franz Ferdinand, the heir to the Austrian throne, in the Bosnian capital, Sarajevo. But Austria's tough ultimatum to Serbia sparked both a geopolitical and a financial chain reaction. As traders and investors suddenly grasped the likelihood of a full-scale European war, with Russia taking the Serbs' side, liquidity was sucked out of the world economy. . . . Perhaps the most remarkable feature of the crisis of 1914 was the closure of the world's major stock markets for up to five months. The Vienna market was the first to close, on July 27. By July 30 all the continental European exchanges had shut their doors. The next day, London and New York felt compelled to follow suit. Although a belated settlement day went smoothly on November 18, the London Stock Exchange did not reopen until January 4. Nothing like this had happened since its foundation in 1773. The New York market reopened for limited trading (bonds for cash only) on Novem-

ber 28, but unrestricted trading did not resume until April 1, 1915.

Imagine not being able to sell your GE stock—or your municipal bonds, or your Treasuries, for that matter. Such an event can't even be called a black swan because it's happened before.

A GAGGLE OF BLACK SWANS

While there is no metric to prove that black swans are appearing more often, I firmly believe that they are. We are experiencing more Knightian uncertainty, more bolts from the blue. And it is my strong belief—though, again, there is no way to prove it—that these bolts will rain on us more frequently. Why?

The first reason is technology. A few people can suddenly affect the lives of many people. Before nuclear weapons, you had to mount an army to kill thousands of people. Now, you can deliver mass destruction in a shipping container or a valise. I am especially worried about the ability of miscreants to affect the power grids of nations like the United States or to wipe banking records clean.

The second reason is information. Yes, abundant and fast-moving information can save lives and prevent economic damage—by, for example, warning people to get out of the way of a hurricane. But such information can also paralyze us, as it did during the volcano-inspired shutdown of air service in Europe and the blowout-inspired shutdown of oil drilling in the Gulf of Mexico. The vast flow of information has made us risk-averse—and at high cost to the economy. My guess is that this kind of demobilizing risk aversion will get worse.

In addition, the more conventional sort of risk also seems to be increasing along with Knightian risk. In 1987, two economists, Dan Galai and Menachem Brener, constructed an index that measured market volatility by examining the prices of stock options on the S&P 500 Index. For more than twenty years, the average value of the options index, maintained by the Chicago Board Options Exchange, has been about twenty. But in October 2008, it spiked to an incredible sixty—a number never seen before. All these factors, taken together, indicate that the world is a far riskier place than it was only twenty years ago.

So, in the face of this uncertainty, what do you do? One rational reaction is to take your chips off the roulette table and walk away. But putting cash under the mattress is a sure way to lose purchasing power to inflation. The truth about investing is that you have to play. In the following chapters, I will show you how.

2

WHAT TO DO: THE STRATEGY

The Margin of Safety strategy is designed to deal with the reality of a world in which risk—both conventional and Knightian—is rising and the growth rate of the U.S. economy is slowing. The strategy is simple: Protect yourself against catastrophic losses while, at the same time, achieve good returns. This chapter presents the basic structure of the strategy; the next two fill in the details. The structure itself has two major themes: first, asset allocation and, second, hedging. Both will almost certainly require big changes in the way you now invest.

ASSET ALLOCATION: DEFAULT TO HALF AND HALF

Many investors own random assets. They like a stock and buy it; ditto, a nice mutual fund a friend has recommended; oh, and what about some gold? Instead of owning stocks, bonds, commodities, real estate, and cash, an investor should own a portfolio—that is, a group of assets, chosen with strategy, structure, foresight, and logic. Nothing in investing—nothing!—is more important than the composition of your portfolio, its asset allocation.

How you allocate your assets is more important than the individual stocks or bonds you choose, and the most powerful element of the Margin of Safety strategy is a new perspective on asset allocation.

Before the events of the past decade, a reasonable asset allocation strategy might be described this way: *Your portfolio should include as high a proportion of stocks as your age and your tolerance of risk can support.* History tells us that stocks return far more than bonds and that, over the long run, stocks are no more risky than bonds (if we define risk as volatility). While stocks might drop, if you hold tight, you'll recoup your losses, and more.

Unfortunately, that approach will no longer work in a world that is changing. Yes, stocks are not for the short run, but, because we cannot be sure of stocks, even in the longer run, some new rules must be heeded as well.

A share of stock is a piece of a corporation. You *share* in the fortunes of the business. The business frequently pays you a dividend as an enticement for you to hang onto your shares (or buy more), and it is this dividend and any increase in the stock's price—owing to expectations of rising profits in the future—that comprise your gains. A bond, on the other hand, represents a much simpler, discrete transaction. It is an IOU, a certificate that reflects a loan an investor makes to a company or a government agency. The lender promises to pay you back over a set period and gives you interest along the way.

There's a significant difference between the interest paid by bonds and the dividends paid by stocks. Bonds pay interest—usually twice a year—in a fixed amount, set at the time the bond is issued. The interest itself, not just the return of principal, is a promise made by the bond issuer. Dividend amounts, by contrast, may be changed by a company at a moment's notice. For example, as the bottom dropped out of the housing market, KB Home, a builder of single-family houses, dropped its dividend from $1 a share in 2007 to 81 cents in 2008 to 25 cents in 2009. Kelly Services, the temporary-employment giant, suspended its dividend entirely in 2009.

Bond investing is also less risky because bondholders, by law, stand in front of stockholders if a company gets into trouble and enters bankruptcy or has to be liquidated. Investors were reminded of this difference, in stark fashion, with the difficulties encountered—even by big businesses like General Motors and AIG—during the 2008–2009 recession.

Stocks and bonds, both of which trade on liquid markets where you can usually buy and sell within seconds, are the two primary assets to hold in a portfolio. Even if you want to own real estate or commodities like gold or agricultural products as a hedge against inflation, you can more conveniently own them through stocks (and, occasionally, corporate bonds) than through owning physical buildings (I have never seen a home as a financial investment, by the way) or futures contracts—or the commodities themselves. So asset allocation comes down to something fairly simple: *What proportion of stocks and bonds should you own in your portfolio?*

To begin, know what your portfolio is *for*. Are you saving to buy a house in five years? Then, considering the volatility of stocks in the short term, you should allocate your assets heavily toward bonds. Are you trying to accumulate enough to send your daughter to college in ten years? Then, you can lean more heavily toward stocks. If you're saving for retirement, consider your age and your other sources of income. The basic question you must ask is this: How will my lifestyle be affected if my portfolio declines by one-third in a year? I hardly need to remind you that it can happen.

THE SHIFT TO BONDS

Because of my concerns about the strength of the U.S. economy and worries about continuing volatility, the Margin of Safety strategy requires that allocations—

across all time horizons—shift from stocks to bonds. For a retirement portfolio, a shift of twenty to thirty percentage points is necessary. Let's take a specific example.

A forty-five-year-old midlevel corporate executive plans to retire at age sixty-five. Besides Social Security, he expects no other retirement income beyond his 401(k) and other investments. My assessment until recently would have been that he should hold 90 percent of his portfolio in stocks and 10 percent in bonds. Then, over the next ten years, he should slowly shift to 80/20 stocks and bonds; then over the next ten, to 70/30 or 60/40 stocks and bonds. Now, under the Margin of Safety strategy, I prescribe a far more conservative allocation plan: 50 percent stocks and 50 percent bonds through the period between age forty-five and sixty-five. On retirement, he should reassess and decide how much income he needs for day-to-day living, but during the accumulation stage, 50/50 is the right proportion.

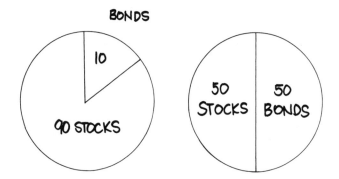

If U.S. growth flattens out—and all indications are that it will—then returns from stocks will probably fall below historic averages. Possibly *far* below. Stocks, remember, are priced based on expected profits over the life of their underlying businesses. If investors assumed that profits would rise by 6 percent a year and now, because of reduced growth, the expectations drop to 3 percent a year, then the stock price will drop—despite the fact that profits will continue to rise.

Bonds, on the other hand, are likely to benefit from lower growth—as long as that growth does not go *too* low. They do, however, carry two kinds of risk. First is credit risk, meaning that the borrower (the corporation or government issuing the bond) might not be able to pay you back. Second is inflation, or interest-rate, risk, meaning that interest rates might rise after you buy the bond.

If interest rates rise, then the price your bond will fetch in the market will fall. That seems counterintuitive, but imagine that you bought a $10,000 bond that matures in ten years with a coupon of 6 percent. The borrower—that is, the seller of the bond—promises to pay you $600 annually for ten years, then to repay the entire $10,000 in principal.

So far, so good. Now, fast-forward one year. Imagine that you want to sell your bond *and* that, because of worries about inflation, the same borrower (the federal government, for instance) must offer ten-year bonds at 7 percent interest, instead of 6 percent interest, to attract lenders. These new bonds pay $700 a year. Obviously, anyone with $10,000 to invest would prefer to buy the bond paying $700 to your bond paying $600, so, to attract buyers, the price of your bond must fall. If it drops to $8,500, then the effective current yield ($600/$8,500) jumps to about 7 percent, so your bond can compete in the marketplace, but you have suffered a loss of $1,500.

Now, understand that this loss in value only applies if you have to *sell* your bond. If you hold it to maturity—the specific date on which the government promised to repay you—then you get the entire face value of the bond, or $10,000. But even if it doesn't seem as if you have lost anything if you wait until maturity, you really have. You have lost the opportunity to earn the higher interest that new bonds are paying.

For this reason, one way to lower the risk in buying bonds (that is, the risk in lending money to a government agency or a corporation) is to choose debt that matures in the short or medium term—say, between two and eight years. That way, if rates rise, you can wait a short time until the bond matures rather than taking a loss. Yes, there is an opportunity cost, but you can fairly quickly take the proceeds and buy a new bond at a higher rate.

In general, when economic growth is modest, there's less chance of inflation, so interest rates are low. In a crisis, investors typically rush to U.S. Treasury bonds as a safe haven from economic storms, again driving down interest rates. But if the U.S. economy gets *very* bad, investors may decide to flee T-bonds because of credit risk—the worry that the American government, like the Argentine, Russian, and Greek governments before it, might not be able to pay the interest and principal. Such an event would be akin to seeing a black swan. It can happen, but the best bet is that bonds will provide more consistent returns than stocks and that, in case of another severe economic downturn, bonds will be hurt less than stocks—and might even be helped.

No one knows for certain about the economy, but the Margin of Safety strategy protects investors against the worst while providing the chance for good gains. Consider history. A portfolio consisting of 90 percent stocks and 10 percent bonds returned an average of 9.6 percent between 1926 and 2009. (In this case, the stocks are represented by the S&P 500 and the bonds by an index of long-term U.S. government debt.) A portfolio split 50/50 between stocks and bonds returned 8.1 percent. So, if history is a guide, you are sacrificing 1½ percentage points by going 50/50. Because my prediction is that the future will be *worse* than the past for U.S. stocks, your sacrifice may be closer to one percentage point a year. But even two points is not too much for insurance against a rotten stock market.

How rotten? A 90/10 stock-bond portfolio has lost as much as 40 percent of its value in a single year while a 50/50 portfolio has *never* lost more than 25 percent. Let's look at five-year holding periods, using Morningstar data. For 90/10 portfolios, the worst loss was an annual average of 10 percent, knocking the value of a $500,000 nest egg down to about $300,000. For 50/50 portfolios, as noted in the Introduction, the loss averaged less than 3 percent, reducing the nest egg to $430,000. Just as important, over ten-year periods, the excess returns from 90/10 portfolios are not so much greater in the best year—a maximum of 18.5 percent versus 17 percent for 50/50 portfolios. So you're not giving up all that much when you default to 50/50.

The Margin of Safety strategy is anchored in a 50/50 rule for investors in their forties, fifties, and sixties. If you're younger, you can afford to increase the proportion of stocks to 70/30—but beware. Only investors who are willing to tolerate a good deal of risk and are putting money away for the very long term should opt for portfolios with stocks representing more than half their assets. The real danger of volatility is that your short-term losses become so psychologically unbearable that you dump your stocks at precisely the wrong time and miss the recovery. The best way to avoid that danger is by maintaining portfolios that don't fluctuate so wildly.

And *maintaining* is the operative word here. You need to rebalance your portfolio every year to bring your investments back to target proportions. Here's an example of what happens if you don't rebalance. Assume a $100,000 portfolio split 50/50 between two low-expense mutual funds issued by Vanguard: for the stock portion, 500 Index; for the bond portion, Long-Term U.S. Treasury.

At the start of 2008, the portfolio had $50,000 in the stock fund and $50,000 in the bond fund. In 2008, stocks fell sharply and bonds rose smartly, so by the end of the year, the portfolio looked like this: $32,000 stocks, $64,000 bonds. Instead of a 50/50 ratio, the proportions are now 34 percent stocks, 66 percent bonds. At this point, you have to rebalance: sell $16,000 worth of bonds and buy $16,000 worth of stocks to bring the ratio back to 50/50.

If you *don't* rebalance at the end of 2008, then, by the end of 2009, your portfolio would be $39,000 in stocks and $49,000 in bonds for a total of $88,000—a loss over the two years of about 12 percent. But if you do rebalance, you would have $58,000 in stocks and $42,000 in bonds for a total of $100,000—breaking even. Then, it's time to rebalance again at the end of 2009, selling about $8,000 in stocks and buying the equivalent in bonds.

Rebalancing is not always as elegantly beneficial as this example indicates, and it does generate capital gains taxes. So try to restrict your rebalancing to tax-deferred accounts, such as IRAs and 401(k) plans, or, better still (if you can afford it), rebalance by buying more stocks or bonds rather than selling one category and buying the other. But it is absolutely necessary to keep your portfolio as stable as you intended when you established the asset allocation in the first place.

It's easier to let a mutual fund manager do the rebalancing—and the stock and bond selecting. Under the rubric *balanced,* many investment firms offer funds that allocate stocks and bonds at a ratio that's close to the norm I suggest. One of the best in recent years has been Mairs & Power Balanced. Despite an expense ratio of 0.8 percent (there's no load, or up-front fee), it has produced an annual average return for investors of 8.7 percent over the fifteen years ending in early December 2010, compared with 6.5 percent for an investment in Vanguard's 500 Index Fund. Just as important, the ride has been relatively smooth. In 2001, when the Vanguard fund linked to the large-cap index fell 12 percent, Mairs & Power Balanced fell only 1 percent; in 2002, the Vanguard index fund dropped 22 percent, but the balanced fund fell only 6 percent. In the disaster of 2008, Mairs & Power Balanced outperformed the Vanguard stock index fund by sixteen percentage points, and when the stock index fund rose 26 percent in 2009, the balanced fund was not too far behind at a gain of 21 percent.

As I write, Mairs & Power Balanced divides its assets this way: 57 percent stocks, 39 percent bonds, and 4 percent cash. But the manager of the fund, William Frels, who has held the job since 1992, has discretion over allocation, not you. The main limitation is that the prospectus calls for having at least one-quarter of the fund's holdings in bonds. Still, this balanced fund—unlike many others—changes its allocations very slowly. I like its style.

BE YOUR OWN HEDGE FUND

One central principle of the Margin of Safety strategy is looking at your economic life as a whole. Most people don't realize it, but they are making a heavy bet on a particular outcome—the equivalent of black on the roulette wheel. Sometimes, however, red comes up. Again and again.

Here's what I mean. When Enron collapsed in 2002, its employees were hit with a double whammy. They lost their jobs and, in many cases, nearly all their retirement funds— because they had invested their money in Enron stock. In financial terms, they had not *hedged*. But Enron employees weren't the only ones who put all their eggs in one basket. Most Americans over the last few decades have done the same thing. They have been *long* on the U.S. economy.

All our investments tend to benefit from the same thing: strong American economic growth. If growth slows, all or nearly all your assets suffer at the same time: The value of your home falls, your stocks decline in value, your corporate and municipal bonds get clobbered, the value of your commodity funds drop (except maybe gold), and, on top of it all, lenders may cut off your lines of credit and your employer may fire you.

What you need are investments whose value *rises*—or at least don't fall too much—when the economy declines. That is, you need a backstop, a hedge against disaster. It's not so difficult, in fact, to be your own hedge fund. Originally, hedge funds were created as protection against bad times, with assets that lacked correlation with the stock market as a whole (that is, assets that tend to move in a different direction from stocks). In recent years, however, many hedge fund managers, seduced by rising stock prices, went *extremely* long on the economy, taking on lots of debt to leverage their profits. Many of those non-hedging hedge funds met disaster. Your own hedge fund should really hedge.

DOWN WITH COORDINATION

The riskiest part of your portfolio is composed of stocks. Therefore, a good way to limit risk is to find other assets that aren't traveling companions to stocks—that is, investments that don't move in tandem with them, either up or down. The financial term is *correlation*. It's a measure between +1.0 and –1.0 that indicates the relationship between the movements of two assets. If there is a perfect relationship, then the correlation is said to be +1.0. If there is no relationship, then it's zero. If there is a perfect *inverse* relationship, then the correlation is –1.0.

Rydex/SGI, an investment firm that specializes in variations on conventional index funds, analyzed correlations with stocks from the start of 2000 to the start of 2010. Here are the firm's most striking conclusions:

- Bonds were utterly uncorrelated to stocks. This finding is precisely what we want to see for the foundation of the Margin of Safety strategy to work: a portfolio roughly half bonds, half stocks, each asset class modulating the ups and downs of the other.

- International stocks were closely coordinated with U.S. stocks, with a correlation of 0.88. In other words, the movement of American equities explains, or accounts for, 88 percent of the movement of foreign equities. Is this a reason to shun foreign stocks? I don't think so. I believe that, in the future, foreign economies—especially in the developing world—will diverge more and more (in a good way!) from the U.S. economy. But the lesson is that broad foreign diversification, especially with stocks in developed markets like Europe and Japan, is not really a significant hedge.

- Standard investments don't offer negative correlations. Only by putting your money on the short side—that is, into things that are specifically geared to go up when the market goes down—do you get consistently inverse movements. Those things are called *derivatives* because their values are *derived* from something extraneous—in this case, stocks.

- Commodities carried a correlation of only +0.2 with U.S. stocks. That may sound counterintuitive since, typically, the prices of commodities, like corn and oil, are driven by consumer and business demand, and a rising stock market usually goes hand in hand with a rising economy and, thus, more buying.

A POWERFUL WAY TO HEDGE

Buying bonds, which aren't closely correlated to stocks, is a good way to hedge. But a more direct—and powerful—method is buying derivatives, which are sophisticated securities whose movements depends on the movement of something else. Over the past decade, money management firms have developed hedging products that are easy for small investors to buy and sell—and, more important, to understand. For example, the management of an exchange-traded fund, or ETF, called ProShares Short S&P 500 buys derivatives that enable it to produce returns that are roughly the *opposite* of the large-cap index, which itself is the benchmark for the U.S. market as a whole. As far as you, the investor, are concerned, the ProShares ETF is like a share of stock whose price moves inversely with the market.

So, in 2008, when the S&P 500 fell 37 percent, the ProShares fund *gained* 39 percent. And in 2009, when the S&P rose 26 percent, the fund *fell* 27 percent. The inverse correlation is not precise, and the folks at ProShares exact a hefty expense ratio of 0.95 percent for their efforts, but the fund offers an significant hedge against disaster.

Imagine a simple $100,000 portfolio: 50 percent large-cap stocks, 40 percent long-term bonds, and 10 percent short-fund hedge. In the average year, the stock portion of the portfolio rises about 10 percent, from $50,000 to $55,000, and the bond portion 5 percent, from $40,000 to $42,000. The short fund loses the inverse of the stocks' gain, so it falls 10 percent, from $10,000 to $9,000.

Final tally: Your hedged portfolio goes from $100,000 to $106,000. Without the hedge, a simple 50/50 portfolio would have risen from $100,000 to $107,500. An all-stock portfolio would have gone to $110,000.

Now, let's take a bad year—stocks lose 40 percent, bonds pay their interest of 5 percent, and the short-fund hedge gains 40 percent. In this case, your $100,000 portfolio—allocated 50/40/10—finishes the year at $86,000. A 50/50 portfolio without the hedge would have ended up at $82,500, and an all-stock portfolio at $60,000.

You can hedge even more with *leveraged* bear funds, such as ProShares UltraShort S&P 500 or Rydex Inverse 2x S&P 500, both of which use debt to move at roughly twice the rate of the stock market, both up and down. Unfortunately, these leveraged funds, for technical reasons, are less reliable in reflecting the double-inverse of the market than the plain-vanilla short funds are in reflecting the single-inverse. For instance, in 2008, ProShares

UltraShort was up only 61 percent (rather than more than 70 percent, as it would have been if it were truly reflecting double the inverse of the S&P); the Rydex offering did better, up 69 percent.

Here's what happens with a leveraged short fund: In the example above of a typical year, instead of rising 6 percent (with a normal short fund), your portfolio rises 5 percent. In the example of a horrific year, instead of dropping 14 percent, your portfolio drops only 10 percent.

Think of these bear funds as insurance policies. Rather than paying a premium every year, you pay it only when stocks go up. Even better, you pay according to how much stocks rise. In a good year for stocks, you'll pay a high premium—but you'll also have more money to pay it. In a bad year, the insurance company gives you a payout—the worse the year, the more you get.

Bear funds are *not* for speculation—which is the way, I'm afraid, most investors use them. Guessing what stocks will do in the short term is a fool's errand. If you really think that stocks are on the brink of decline in the next month or two, my suggestion is for you to take a deep breath and forget it or else to do the opposite (vice versa if you think stocks will zoom in the very short term). If you're a typical investor, your suspicions—which are based on your fears or enthusiasms—are more likely to be wrong than right. Bear funds are to prevent calamity, and that's quite enough for a day's work.

COMMODITIES

For most investors, commodities are derivatives, too. You aren't really buying or selling corn or platinum; you are trading a contract to purchase those things on a specific date. You don't really want to take delivery of a truckload of pork bellies. During the decade ending in 2009, commodities, as represented by the S&P Goldman Sachs Commodity Index, proved to have low correlations not just with stocks but also with bonds (+0.3). In 2007, for instance, with large-cap stocks up just 5 percent, the commodity index rose 32 percent. But commodities were no help in 2008, losing more than 30 percentage points, just seven fewer points than stocks.

I will admit to being baffled by commodities—in part because they constitute an asset class that is so varied as to be nearly impossible to define. What do oil, oats, copper, and pork bellies have in common? They are all *things,* or commodities, but they don't move up, roughly in unison, the way that most stocks and bonds tend to do over time. There's no real consensus on what a commodity basket looks like, so during 2009—to pick a year—the three major commodity indexes gained 13, 19, and 26 percent. Quite a variation.

In addition, it is difficult for the small investor to buy commodities. Purchasing futures contracts, which involve massive leverage and the possibility of margin calls if prices go down, is far too risky for most of us. Alternatives have developed in recent years—such as managed futures limited partnerships—that are either too opaque or give too much discretion to managers. The best way to buy futures is through an index fund like iShares S&P GSCI Commodity-Indexed Trust, which is linked to the Goldman index. This ETF, started in July 2006, has only a brief track record, carries an expense ratio that's high for an index fund at 0.75 percent, and is heavily weighted toward energy (70 percent of the portfolio!). PowerShares DB Commodity Index Tracking, another ETF, has similar longevity and expenses, but, linked with the Deutsche Bank Liquid Commodity Index, has an energy weighting of only 55 percent.

PUTTING IT TOGETHER

The Margin of Safety strategy has no place for commodities, either through individual contracts or funds. You can capitalize on rising prices of things by owning shares of energy, forest products, or agribusiness companies. No need to add unnecessary complexity.

Chapter 6 recommends specific portfolios for investors of particular ages, with particular needs and risk-aversion profiles. But for now, let me modify the 50/50 rule of thumb. Everyone needs not only bonds but also a further hedge based on derivatives. You can decide yourself, or with your investment advisor, which hedges to own: I have made the case for bear funds, and, in Chapter 4, I will go into detail on three other uses of derivatives to hedge.

So, the new allocation for a typical investor looks like this: 50 percent stocks, 40 percent bonds, and 10 percent derivative hedges. Now, we're ready for the fun part: *which* stocks and, after that, *which* bonds and hedges.

3

WHAT TO DO: STOCKS

The Margin of Safety strategy calls for reducing the proportion of stocks in your portfolio. The stocks that remain should fall into four broad categories: stocks that pay substantial and consistent dividends, value stocks, small- and micro-cap stocks, and the stocks of aspiring economies. Let's look at each one of these in detail.

PAYING DIVIDENDS

When a business makes a profit, it has a choice: Return some of the money to investors or keep it all to plow back into the company. From the 1950s through the 1980s, the companies that make up the S&P 500 paid out an average of half their earnings to investors in the form of dividends. Then, the payout ratio started to decline. By the mid-2000s, it had dropped to only one-third of earnings.

In 1980, 31 of the S&P 500 companies paid no dividend at all; by 2003, the figure had jumped to 115.

Dividends fell out of favor for two reasons: First, they are taxed twice. If a business makes $1,000, it pays a corporate tax (typically, around 35 percent) on the profit. Then, if the business distributes the remaining $650 to investors, they, too, have to pay taxes. The federal tax on those dividends dropped in 2003 to 15 percent, but that change still left investors with only about $550 out of the $1,000 the business earned before taxes. The rate is currently scheduled to rise to as much as 40 percent by 2013, and don't forget the bite that states take. Of course, dividends have always been taxed twice, but in recent years economic research started to show that, partly because of that taxation, investors didn't care one way or the other whether they received a dividend. The managers of corporations were only too happy to keep the profits, reinvesting them to make their businesses bigger. (A CEO of a company with revenues of $10 billion, after all, typically makes a larger salary than a CEO of a company with revenues of $5 billion.)

The second reason for the decline in dividends is more emotional. In the 1990s, exciting high-tech companies emerged on the scene that paid no dividends and didn't intend to. Instead, they hoarded the cash they earned— not because they needed it for capital investment in their own businesses but because they wanted to buy other companies and, in a way, they wanted to show off.

A stock that paid no dividend became, practically by definition, a hot growth stock. Managers whose stocks paid dividends seemed to be admitting that they weren't good stewards of their investors' money; they couldn't put it to use in high-powered ways. Also, stock prices shot up at a faster rate than dividend increases. As a result, dividend yields plummeted even as companies were earning record profits. The average yield for the large-cap stocks of the S&P 500 dropped from about 5 percent between 1975 and 1985 to about 3 percent between 1985 and 1995 to a mere 1.1 percent by 2000. But, with the tech crash and the high volatility of the decade, the attractions of dividends became much more evident, and yields began to rise again.

Microsoft exemplifies this phenomenon. The software company went public in 1986 and didn't start paying dividends until 2003, a year in which its balance sheet showed $49 billion in cash and no debt. By October 2010, the company's stock carried a yield (annual dividend divided by stock price) of 2.4 percent.

At a time when ten-year Treasury bonds were yielding 3.2 percent, a dividend of 2.4 percent was not too shabby. But there are loads of other good, solid companies with yields considerably higher: Merck, the giant pharmaceutical house, at 4.3 percent; DuPont, chemicals, 3.4 percent; Consolidated Edison, New York's electric utility, 4.9 percent; Verizon, telecom, 5.9 percent; Automatic Data Processing, payroll outsourcing, 3.1 percent; RPM International, rustproofing, 4.1 percent.

But why *shouldn't* stocks yield more than Treasuries? Aren't stocks riskier? Yes, they are, but stock dividends aren't fixed. Certainly, they can go down, but they usually go up. Clorox, for example, pays a dividend of $2.20 a share. With the stock priced at $62 in December 2010, that's a yield of 3.5 percent. But if Clorox raises its payout 5 percent annually, then in fifteen years, the dividend will rise to $4.56, so the yield, based on an original investment at $68, will jump to 6.7 percent. A T-bond maturing in fifteen years, which in December 2010 was paying around 3.5 percent interest, will continue paying the same 3.5 percent throughout its life. (By the way, Clorox has increased its dividend for the last twenty-seven years in a row, and over the past fifteen years, the dividend has *quadrupled*.)

The history of yields shows that, when investors get scared, they demand higher payouts. During the late 1800s and the early twentieth century, dividend yields were roughly equivalent to interest rates on long-term Treasuries. Then, as stock prices rose in the 1920s, yields fell. After the Crash in 1929, yields rose again—and stayed at high levels, even higher than T-bonds, until the 1950s. Then, once more, they began a slow and steady decline until the bear markets of the first decade of the twenty-first century, when they started rising again. Today, compared with bond interest, dividend yields of high-quality companies are more enticing than they have been in half a century.

SHOW ME THE MONEY

The attraction of dividends begins with cash in hand. Rather than promises of capital gains at some point in the future, you get a share of the profits every three months—money you can use to pay your own expenses or reinvest in the company that paid the dividend, or somewhere else.

Dividends also have less evident delights. First, they provide visibility into the faith with which managers view their firms' future. No CEO wants to cut a dividend, so payouts are set conservatively, with management saying, in effect, "The way we see our business, we think we can give you a dollar a year as far as the eye can see, and we'll try to raise that a bit each year." A CEO with doubts would limit the dividend to, say, 50 cents. As a result, I believe that dividends are a better indicator of corporate health than any other metric.

A dividend is also an indicator of a stock's valuation—that is, whether it is cheap or expensive. The denominator of a dividend yield, remember, is a share's price. If the numerator—the annual dividend payout—stays the same, and the price falls, then the yield will rise. So, often, a high yield—especially a high yield that is *rising*—signifies a bargain, just as a low price-to-earnings ratio does.

While a dividend yield shows the cash a company is giving investors as a percentage of what the investors pay for its stock, an "earnings yield" shows a company's paper profits as a percentage of the stock price. An earnings yield is the inverse of a stock's price-to-earnings, or P/E, ratio. For instance, a P/E of 16 is equivalent to an earnings yield of 6.3 percent. Both dividend yield and earnings yield are important valuation metrics, but I would argue that the dividend yield tells you more. After all, you can pocket cash, but you can't necessarily pocket the earnings a company reports. A chunk of those earnings, for instance, goes to capital reinvestment—building a new plant or buying new machines.

The notion of dividend yield as signal of good value is so strong that it spawned an entire investing strategy: the Dogs of the Dow, developed in 1978 by Michael O'Higgins, who set up a money management firm to help clients profit from it. You invest equal amounts each year in the ten stocks with the highest yields among the thirty stocks in the Dow Jones Industrial Average. Then, a year later, you sell those stocks and repeat the process with the new top ten–yielding stocks. O'Higgins considered these stocks "dogs" because their lofty yields indicated that investors were shunning them; that is, they were cheap.

James O'Shaughnessy, an investment advisor based in Connecticut, tested the Dogs against actual results from 1952 to 1996 and found they beat the S&P 500 by an average of 3.5 percentage points a year—a powerful performance. Investors thronged to the Dogs of the Dow, and brokerage firms even set up unit trusts to profit from them. Alas, in the mid-1990s, the system stopped working. The Dow as a whole whipped the Dogs by two full points, on average, for the fifteen years ending 2009. The Dogs didn't even provide protection against a bear market. In 2008, they fell 42 percent—a worse showing than both the Dow 30 and the S&P 500.*

What happened? Perhaps so many investors piled into the Dogs just before they were reset each year that prices were driven up artificially, making good returns hard to come by. A better explanation may be that the quarter-century O'Shaughnessy studied was a fluke, and the Dow list, which has tended in the past to be heavy on financials and utilities, is so lacking in diversification that distorted results should be expected.

A high dividend yield, after all, can be a sign of danger. When the denominator (the price) drops sharply, pushing up the percentage yield, that price decline often indicates that a company is in trouble and may soon have to cut, or even eliminate, its dividend. In July 2008, for example, Bank of America Corp. was trading at $21 a share and paying an annual dividend of $2.56, for a yield of 12.2 percent—more than double its usual rate. Definitely a warning! Sure enough, in December, the financial giant slashed its dividend in half and, in March 2009 cut it to just 4 cents.

Understand that when a service like Yahoo! Finance or

---

* For more than you could possibly want to know about the Dogs of the Dow, see this eponymous website: www.dogsofthedow.com.

Morningstar lists the yields of stocks, those percentages are based on the "indicated" dividends—that is, annual dividends computed from what the companies *have been* paying. Poor profits, especially for a firm that dispenses a large proportion of its earnings as dividends (also known as the *payout ratio*), are a good indicator that a dividend will shortly be slashed.

While buying all the Dogs of the Dow is not a viable strategy, it is worth looking at high-yielding stocks on the Dow each year—to glean suggestions for your own selections. For example, among the latest Dogs, I view Kraft Foods (yielding 3.7 percent in December and ranking fourth-highest at the start of 2010), McDonald's (3.1 percent), and Boeing (2.6 percent) as standouts.

Perhaps even more important than a high yield is a dividend that rises consistently. A company that can increase its payout year after year may have a "moat" around it—something special that wards off competition that depletes profits. A moat might be a set of patents, a strong brand name, a loyal customer base, or simply a brilliant management methodology.

ENTER THE ARISTOCRATS

Standard & Poor's maintains an index that it calls Dividend Aristocrats. These are large-caps on the S&P 500 that have increased their dividends annually for at least twenty-five years. There were forty-three companies on the 2010 list—a resilient bunch that, unlike such vaunted businesses as General Electric, Pfizer, and Gannett, managed to keep boosting their payouts to investors even in the recession of 2008–2009.

Who are these Aristocrats? Household names predominate, a strong indication of the power of brand as moat. There's Procter & Gamble, for example, which has increased its dividend for fifty-three years straight, as of the end of 2009. There's Johnson & Johnson, at forty-seven years; Coca-Cola, also forty-seven; Walmart Stores, thirty-five; McDonald's, thirty-three; Clorox, thirty-two.*

If a company consistently raises its dividend, and if you hold the stock long enough, the annual yield on your original investment can become sensational—far more than the Clorox example. Imagine that you bought 100 shares of P&G stock in March 1995. It was trading at $12.50 a share (adjusted for later splits) with a dividend of 40 cents for the year. So the dividend yield was 3.2 percent (.40/12.50 = 0.032). You pocket $40 in cash annually.

Now, fast-forward. The dividend has been rising, bit by bit, for fifteen years. In 2010, it reached $1.93 per share. So now you pocket $193 on your original investment of $1,250. That is a return, from your dividend alone, of 15 percent (1.93/12.50 = 0.15). Fifteen percent in a single

---

* For a website dedicated to the Dividend Aristocrats, go to: www.dividend aristocrats.net. Another good site, focusing on stocks with rising dividends, is at: www.dividendgrowthinvestor.com.

year—a year during which ten-year Treasury bonds were yielding less than 3 percent. If the past fifty-three years are any indication, the dividend—and your annual yield—will continue to rise. And, while P&G's dividend was rising, its stock wasn't standing still. Shares quintupled in value over the fifteen-year period.

P&G is not even the most spectacular example I could have chosen. Consider Walmart. In 1995, its annual dividend, adjusted for splits, was just a penny a share. Today, it's $1.21. In 1995, McDonald's was paying a dividend of 13 cents on a stock trading at $14; that's a yield of less than 1 percent. Today, the dividend is $2.44 a share, or an annual return, from dividend alone, of 17 percent on the original investment of fifteen years ago.

How have companies with long-term rising dividends performed as a whole? Very, very well. At the end of 2009, the S&P Dividend Aristocrats had beaten the S&P as a whole over the previous fifteen years by a margin of 10.7 percent to 8 percent. The Aristocrats also beat the S&P over three-, five-, and ten-year periods, and came out ahead in seven of the last ten years. A fluke like the Dogs? It can't be ruled out, but, in my view, the concept behind the Aristocrats is much sounder. And the portfolio is much broader.

Just as important, for followers of the Margin of Safety strategy, the Aristocrats were considerably less risky than the average S&P stock. Two-thirds of Aristocrats received quality ratings of A or A+ from S&P, compared with one-fourth of the S&P as a whole. Standard deviation—a measure of a stock's volatility—was lower. Over the past five years, it was just 15 percent, compared with 20 percent for the S&P 500. And look at bear markets: Between 2000 and 2002, while the S&P was dropping an average of 14 percent a year, the Aristocrats actually rose 3 percent. In 2008, the S&P fell 37 percent, but the Aristocrats fell only 22 percent.

The Aristocrats provide Margin of Safety investors with a delicious shopping list. Of the forty-three, my own top ten would include these:

- Procter & Gamble, the world's top consumer-goods company, with such brands as Tide, Gillette, and Charmin.

- C. R. Bard, maker of medical devices, such as catheters. It's a very consistent earner, yielding only 0.8 percent in early December 2010 but with steady increases annually.

- ExxonMobil, a broadly diversified energy company, now making a large bet on natural gas. Dividends have risen twenty-seven years in a row, yielding 2.4 percent.

- Target, a well-run firm, though, like all retailers, subject to volatility based on the economy. Still, annual dividend rises give confidence. Yields 1.7 percent.

- Eli Lilly, a pharmaceutical company with such drugs as Cymbalta and Cialis. Track record for conservative performance, yielding 5.7 percent, about 1.5 points greater than a thirty-year Treasury bond.

- Leggett & Platt, maker of components for everyday products, like springs for beds. Subject to dips in recessions, but still relatively steady, yielding 4.9 percent.

- Chubb, the eleventh-largest property and casualty insurer in the United States, catering to higher-end clients. It has a strong balance sheet, yielding 2.5 percent.

- Pepsico, maker of brands such as Lay's, Tropicana, and Quaker (as well as Pepsi), with a powerful distribution system, yielding 3 percent.

- Cintas, a renter of work uniforms and a newcomer on the Aristocrats list. One of my long-time favorites, it has beaten the S&P by an average of three percentage points annually for the past decade. Yielding 1.7 percent.

- Archer Daniels Midland, the giant processor of agricultural products. Dividend up 50 percent in four years, now yielding 2 percent.

You can buy a variation on the Dividend Aristrocats by owning an ETF called SPDR S&P Dividend. The fund, launched only in 2005, has a portfolio that includes the fifty highest-yielding stocks among the companies in the S&P 1500 (a supercomposite that includes mid-caps and small-caps as well as large-caps) that have raised their dividends for at least twenty-five years in a row. The fund yields 3.3 percent, and its expense ratio is a mere 0.35 percent, but it is riskier than both the Aristrocrats and the S&P 500.

Another excellent choice for a Margin of Safety portfolio is Vanguard's Dividend Appreciation ETF, based on the Broad Dividend Achievers Index, which includes about 200 stocks—from all three major U.S. exchanges (NYSE, NASDAQ, and Amex), an even wider universe than the S&P 1500—that have increased their dividends for at least ten years in a row. Launched in 2006, the fund beat the S&P by ten points in the down year of 2008 and was beaten by seven points in the up year of 2009. It carries an expense ratio of 0.2 percent and is less risky than the S&P offering, but its yield in December 2010 was only 2 percent.

As further evidence that dividend-paying stocks are managed conservatively, the top ten holdings of the Vanguard fund have an average price-to-earnings ratio of just sixteen. In other words, you pay just $16 for every dollar of a stock's profits. As a rough rule, a P/E in the teens or below is often a good buy at a time when interest rates are low (when, for instance, the ten-year Treasury bond yields less than 5 percent). Among the attractive stocks in the Vanguard portfolio: Chevron, an energy stock yielding

3.3 percent, and Abbott Laboratories, a pharmaceutical stock yielding 3.8 percent.

Another ETF, PowerShares High-Yield Dividend Achievers, follows a methodology similar to that of the Vanguard fund, first finding stocks that have raised dividends each year for the last decade, then picking only the fifty highest-yielding stocks. As a result, the overall yield is higher, and the ride a bit bumpier, since some of the high-yielding stocks are low-priced for a reason. A fourth ETF, iShares Dow Jones Select Dividend Index, adds another wrinkle, using a screen that restricts its portfolio to companies with a payout ratio of no more than 60 percent (that is, the companies distribute less than three-fifths of their earnings to shareholders—offering what would seem to be a margin of safety). The fund also requires a dividend payout that is either flat or rising and a relatively high yield. The iShares fund has been a huge disappointment, trailing the S&P 500 badly, with higher risk. I take two lessons from this: First, a relatively low payout ratio is not a significant plus (perhaps because managers of such companies are skittish about offering their shareholders too much cash—a sign of a lack of confidence), and, second, allowing stocks with a *flat* dividend to pass the screen admits too many potential laggards to the club. Stick with a simple rising-dividend strategy.

If you are looking for individual stocks that pay high dividends, a good place to start is the *Value Line Invest-*

ment Survey, a weekly subscription service (also online, of course) that's my favorite research tool. In each issue, *Value Line* publishes a list of the hundred highest-yielding stocks from among the thousands it covers. Scan the list, searching especially for companies with ratings of at least average (3, where 1 is tops and 5 is worst) for timeliness and safety. There are bargains here, but be picky. For example, looking at a recent list, I was intrigued by such companies as Kinder Morgan Energy Partners, an oil and gas pipeline partnership, with a yield of 6.3 percent; New York Community Bancorp, a thrift, at 5.7 percent; and Vodafone Group, telecom, 3.5 percent. I was troubled by the 10.1 percent yield for World Wrestling Entertainment. It's just too high; the company is struggling in a bad economy.

Between 1926 and 2009, dividends accounted for 34 percent of the total return of stocks. But that proportion has bounced around over the years. In the 1970s, dividends represented half of stocks' total return; in the 1990s, just one-seventh. The tide seems to be turning, and, as more investors come to understand the joy of dividends, the stocks that pay them consistently will begin to rise. You would think they would be priced at a premium— and they may be someday. For now, you should enjoy the discount, and take your rewards.

GRAHAM'S MARGIN OF SAFETY

Much of the appeal of stocks that pay good dividends is their relative security. They hand you cash frequently, and, by definition, their yields indicate value. They have, in other words, a margin of safety. That phrase, as I noted in the Introduction, comes from the great financier Benjamin Graham, who, in collaboration with David Dodd, wrote the classic *Security Analysis* in 1934. In Graham's definition, a margin of safety was the difference between a stock's "intrinsic" value and its market price. In other words, investors should look for stocks that are bargains—stocks that are trading for less than they are truly worth.

A blinding flash of the obvious? Certainly, everyone loves a bargain, but Graham was searching not just for good deals but for *extremely* good deals—because "the buyer of bargain issues places particular emphasis on the ability of the investment to withstand adverse developments." In Graham's time, there were companies that were trading for less than their net working capital (current assets minus all liabilities, including long-term debt and preferred stock) or even for less than the value of their cash and short-term securities, minus any debt. Such companies actually existed in the 1930s, when investors stampeded from stocks. Today, it's difficult, if not impossible, to find them. Still, it is not hard to find stocks that meet one of Graham's principal criteria—that the earnings yield (remember, that's the inverse of the P/E ratio) be less than the yield on long-term bonds. Even if ten-year Treasury bonds go to 5 percent, a P/E of under 20 would meet Graham's standard.

The Margin of Safety strategy does not hew strictly to Grahamism, but we do love a bargain! A good place to begin a search for Graham-style equities is another list each week in *Value Line*—"Bargain Basement Stocks," defined as having P/E multiples and net working capital ratios that fall in the bottom fourth of the research firm's universe. (Unfortunately, it is rare these days to find *any* company on the list that has net working capital per share that's lower than its stock price.)

On a recent list, the most attractive stock was Tech Data, a distributor of information-technology products, at a price-to-net working capital ratio of 143 percent. At the time, its balance sheet (Morningstar's Web site, the best source, gives you ten years of statistics) showed $1.1 billion in cash and $400 million in debt. That's net cash of $700 million—a large sum for a company whose market capitalization is $2.2 billion. Tech Data is a profitable company, ranked above average for timeliness and average for safety by *Value Line*, and it trades at a forward P/E, based on projections of its 2010 earnings, of 10 and a price that's equal to its book value, or net worth on the balance sheet.

Also high on the Bargain Basement list is an old favorite of mine, National Presto Industries, with a top (1) rating for timeliness—that is, *Value Line* sees strong price appreciation twelve months ahead—and, again, average for safety. The company is in the mundane business of making popcorn poppers, salad mixers, and pressure cookers. It has $167 million in cash and readily marketable short-term investments (about 20 percent of its market cap) and no debt at all. Net income has increased, despite the recession, for five years in a row, but the company trades at a forward P/E ratio of just 12.

THE EFFICIENT MARKET HYPOTHESIS

In 1970, economist Eugene Fama coined the term *efficient market hypothesis* in a scholarly journal article. He argued that, since the price of a stock at this moment is determined by everything that could be possibly be known about it right now—including probabilities about events that are likely to happen in future—its price is "efficient," or as accurate as it can be at this instant. For example, if investors understood, to the point of certainty, that a firm would, two years from now, develop new software that could instantly translate Mandarin into English to perfection, then the price of that firm's stock would reflect the likely future profits gleaned from the software today. Those profits would be accounted for, discounted to their present value, in today's stock price.

In other words, the EMH contends that a stock's price

tomorrow is unknown from today's perspective. Thus, stocks move in what Burton Malkiel of Princeton called a "random walk," meandering in ways that can't be predicted.* Few investors should be able to perform better than the market as a whole over long periods and those that do are more likely to be lucky than smart. When John Bogle, founder of the Vanguard Group, said that he knew no one who could consistently predict what the market will do in the short term (see the Introduction), he was making the case for index funds, and it's a good one.

But the truth is that some people *can* beat the market, and they do it by discovering those rare instances where the market is *not* efficient. Graham concocted the image of Mister Market, a manic-depressive who gets far too enthusiastic about stocks and bids them up too high, then gets too gloomy and won't buy them at any price. As Warren Buffett once said, "The true investor welcomes volatility . . . because a wildly fluctuating market means that irrationally low prices will periodically be attached to solid businesses." The operative word is *irrationally*. The truth is that markets do become irrational about certain stocks, presenting investors with glorious opportunities. The fact that the market is efficient most of the time doesn't mean it's efficient *all* the time.

---

* The phrase comes from Malkiel's classic, *A Random Walk Down Wall Street*, first published in 1973.

FINDING WHAT'S CHEAP

The long-term history of the stock market indicates that there is one kind of stock that seems to defy the EMH: the value stock. The simplest way is to define it is through specific ratios, such as price-to-earnings (P/E), price-to-book-value (P/B), price-to-cash-flow (P/CF), price-to-sales (P/S) or dividend yield. All these indicators are important. There is no single key to discovering value, but I do have my favorite metric.

In its own analysis, Morningstar, the research firm, uses price-to-book—that is, the ratio of a stock's share price to its net worth on the balance sheet per share. The firm divides stocks into two simple categories by P/B: Those in the top half are considered growth stocks; those in the bottom, value stocks. Over the most recent forty-year period, value *clobbered* growth by 2.5 percentage points annually, on average. For smaller stocks, the gap was even wider. Value mid-caps beat growth mid-caps by 4.2 points; for the smallest stocks, the difference was an amazing 6.3 points.

Typically, investors trade risk for return. A low-risk security like a short-term Treasury note will return a good deal less than a high-tech stock, but the T-note has less volatility and less chance of becoming worthless. With value stocks, however, you get *both* higher returns than the stock market as a whole and lower risk. Overall, standard deviation for value was 2.9 percentage points lower than for growth.

In his extensive study of investment styles, *What Works on Wall Street,* James O'Shaughnessy examined fifty-two years of stock data (ending in 2003) and concluded that value indicators were signposts to success. Stocks with low P/E ratios narrowly beat those with average P/E ratios, but stocks with low P/B ratios did even better, and, surprisingly enough, low P/S turned out to be the "king of the value factors," exceeding the market as a whole by an annual average of three percentage points. You might wonder why sales is a factor at all in valuing a stock. Aren't profits what count? Ultimately, yes, but think of it this way: Imagine a company whose sales are strong, but whose profits are weak. Such a company might be ripe for a change in management. The new team could cut costs and produce more profits out of the same revenues. Whatever the reason, a P/S ratio of 1 or lower is often an indicator of a great deal.

But a bigger question is why the value-stock anomaly exists at all. Why should a group of stocks produce higher profits at lower risk? The answer seems to lie in investor psychology. When people see a stock with a low valuation, they naturally want to stay away. It must be a lousy company. Investors seek comfort in crowds, so they go with the hot item, the star of the moment. The Margin of Safety strategy gives investors the security—through their bonds and their hedges—to take more chances with some of their stock selections. Of course, you really *aren't* taking more chances when you buy value stocks. It just looks that way.

All the indicators of value have drawbacks. Earnings, for instance, may bounce up and down. A current P/E ratio, based on the last twelve months of earnings, may have been overtaken by events, but a forward P/E ratio (preferred by many analysts) has to be based on a prediction of the year ahead, which could be wildly inaccurate. Book value and sales tend to be steadier and, perhaps for that reason, more meaningful. Still, book value may include questionable assets, such as inventory that will never be sold, and it's difficult to compare P/S ratios across industries—a retailer, say, with a software firm. Walmart recently earned $15 billion in profits on $417 billion in sales while Microsoft earned $19 billion on just $62 billion in sales.

I like to look at all the indicators, but my favorite is P/B. Again, *Value Line* provides a meaningful list each week. Stay away from retailers because of distortions caused by inventory (clothes in stores, for instance, are carried as assets but sometimes have to be drastically marked down) and scan for companies that have at least average safety rankings, positive earnings, and a low P/E ratio as well as a P/B under 1.5. An example is SkyWest, a regional air carrier, trading at a P/B of 0.6—that is, its price is 40 percent lower than its net worth on the balance sheet. It trades at a P/S of 0.4, P/CF of 2.6, and a forward P/E of 11.

This stock is cheap! And it even pays a dividend, which has been rising steadily from a penny a year in 1990 to 16 cents in 2010.

Or consider The Finish Line, a chain of almost 700 stores that sell sporting wear, like running shoes and warm-up jackets with an array of value metrics: forward P/E of 14, P/S of 0.9, P/CF of 6.6. The company has lots of cash ($235 million, or about one-fourth of market cap) and no debt—great attributes in a time of turmoil. Best of all, with The Finish Line you may be getting a company that's priced as a value stock but growing like a growth stock. *Value Line* projects that over the next five years, earnings will increase at 21 percent annually on average, cash flow at 14 percent, and dividends at 17 percent. Sorry to throw so many figures at you, but just pick one: If earnings rise at 15 percent a year instead of 21 percent, then in five years, The Finish Line will double its profits. That will mean that an investor today will be getting a yearly earnings return on his investment in the company of more than 15 percent. Compare that with a 3 percent bond. Ben Graham would be pleased!

Of course, there are no guarantees. The Finish Line's earnings plummeted from $62 million in 2005 to $16 million in 2007. Bad things happen to good companies. Also, understand that stocks don't stay in the value category forever. As they gain popularity and their valuations rise, they can move into the growth category—and perhaps back to value again. In the case of The Finish Line, should its price suddenly jump by 50 percent, the stock would no longer fall under the value rubric, and you should sell. Already, I am watching the rising P/B ratio, now at 2.

Rather than conducting your own search for value and selling when the definition no longer applies, you can own funds that do the work for you. Index funds geared to value abound. For instance, iShares Morningstar Large Value Index fund, an ETF, selects value stocks using a formula that includes all the usual subjects: P/E, P/B, and so on. Its only drawback is a small portfolio (seventy-four stocks), which can cause volatility. Another ETF, SPDR Dow Jones Large Cap Value (which also comes in small- and mid-cap versions), defines value stocks as having relatively low revenue and earnings growth. Its portfolio contains more than 300 stocks, led by ExxonMobil and P&G. Both these ETFs have expenses in the quarter-point range.

Because the Efficient Market Hypothesis (again, the notion that stocks are accurately priced for the moment) does not operate as robustly in this category, value is an area where smart stock pickers have an edge. One of my favorites is Donald Yacktman, whose eponymous fund beat the S&P by eleven points in 2008 and by at least twenty points in each of the other recent down years, 2000, 2001, and 2002. Yacktman owns only about forty stocks and keeps them practically forever. Among the top holdings are wallflowers like Clorox, plus several media companies, including Comcast and Viacom. Plus Microsoft! (Now, there's a stock that has switched from growth to value. In the 1990s, it carried a P/E in the 30s and 40s. But toward the end of 2010, its forward P/E was 10.) The Yacktman fund's performance is nothing short of phenomenal. Over ten years, Yacktman has beaten the S&P by an annual average of 11 points, and it charges expenses of 0.9 percent, a bargain.

Another approach to value is to buy not merely stocks that are overlooked because they're dull—like Pepsi—but also stocks that are truly beaten up because they are in sectors Mister Market hates. Analysts for Raymond James Associates, led by Anthony Pollini, were high on banks in early 2010, even with a sluggish economy persisting and with bank failures set to exceed those of 2009. "We believe bank stocks still have plenty of upside potential," they wrote, "given the recent P/E level" plus a projected increase in earnings of 25 percent annually for the next three years.

At the time of the analysts' report, in March 2010, the forward P/E ratio for Goldman Sachs, perhaps the strongest U.S. bank of all, was a mere 9; for JPMorgan Chase, 10; and for New York Community, which I cited earlier in this chapter for its juicy yield, 12. The analysts were particularly enamored of Wells Fargo, Bank of America, First Financial of Ohio, and Tower Bancorp of Pennsylvania. I cite this example not necessarily to urge you to buy banks right now but to look closely at sectors others don't want to touch. Also, realize that getting timing right is nearly impossible. By the fall of 2010, Goldman Sachs had fallen another twenty points, and its P/E had dropped to 8. Other sectors that were unloved in late 2010 were trucking and newspapers. Will newspapers ever come back? Not as they were, but a few companies, including the *Washington Post* (which now earns more of its profits from education services than from publishing) and Gannett (with a forward P/E of 7 but a lot of debt) seem to be adapting to the tough new environment.

BUY ASPIRING MARKETS

In Chapter 1, I argued that developing, or aspiring, markets, like China, India, and Brazil, were outstripping developed, or mature, ones like the United States, France, and Japan. In the past, aspiring markets were an afterthought. But today, the Margin of Safety strategy considers them essential. Because the world is changing, your portfolio must include a healthy dose of stocks from countries whose Gross Domestic Product per capita is still low—below $12,000, or about one-fourth that of the United States—but whose growth rates are impressive.

At the end of 2009, I asked Morningstar to do a computer run to select the top-performing stocks of the past ten years, limiting the universe to companies that are listed on the New York Stock Exchange and the NASDAQ Stock Market and have a market capitalization (the number of all traded shares multiplied by the stock price) of at least $1 billion. The top three stocks available on U.S. domestic exchanges turned out to be Brazilian!

Number one was Gerdau, a steel producer with sales throughout Latin America. In second place was Tele Norte Leste Holding, a telecom company, focused on domestic Brazilian consumers. In third was Braskem SA, a maker of specialty chemicals, mainly for the Brazilian market. Gerdau's stock price rose an annual average of 29 percent, meaning that a $10,000 investment increased to $127,000—what Peter Lynch, the fabled former manager of Fidelity Contrafund, would call a "12-bagger."

In all, 16 of the 100 best performers were American Depositary Receipts, or ADRs (that is, U.S. shares of foreign companies) of firms based in aspiring nations—not just in Brazil but also China, Chile, Russia, and Mexico. Latin America was the standout for mutual funds as well as individual stocks. When Morningstar ranked geographical fund categories for five-year performance through 2010, China region funds were far and away the best, with average returns of 19 percent a year; Latin American funds were next at 16 percent, followed by Pacific/Asia (without Japan) funds at 12 percent. The best U.S. fund category was natural resources at 8 percent, followed by technology at 6 percent.

After such spectacular performance, you might expect developing markets to take a breather—and they might, for a short time. No stock, or sector, goes straight up, and aspiring markets have a penchant for volatility. The Aberdeen Indonesia Fund, for instance, has a standard deviation of 42 percent, indicating that it's twice as volatile as the U.S. stock market. In 2003, the fund tripled, and in 2009, it fell by more than half.

But over the longer term, you would be foolish to ignore these markets. Also, investing in such stocks has become much easier than it was a decade ago. You can choose ADRs or foreign stocks directly listed on U.S. exchanges, like Petrobras Energía, the Brazilian oil and gas company; you can ask your broker to buy shares that trade only on foreign markets; or you can opt for portfolios of emerging-markets stocks—mutual funds, closed-end funds, and exchange-traded funds.

GOING DOMESTIC WHILE GOING FOREIGN

The problem with the larger portfolios, like Vanguard Emerging Stock Index fund, is that they tend to own larger, supply-side companies—exporters like South Korea's Samsung or Israel's Teva Pharmaceuticals (in my view, Korea and Israel have graduated from developing-market status, anyway). I prefer a fund like AIM Developing Markets, which is more focused on domestic markets within aspiring economies and has top holdings like Banco Bradesco, a spectacular performer in recent years that caters to the financial needs of low- and middle-income Brazilians; Siam Commercial Bank (Thailand); and Naspers, a South Africa–based media company with interests in sub-Saharan Africa and other developing markets, like India, China, and Brazil. Standard & Poor's gives its best rating to Lazard Emerging Markets Equity Portfolio, a mutual fund whose stocks include Redecard, a Brazilian company that offers credit cards to consumers and electronic payment services to businesses, and Egypt-based Orascom Construction, with large industrial and commercial projects in the Middle East and North Africa.

If you want to concentrate on China, there are some excellent new domestic-focused choices among exchange-traded and closed-end funds, which trade just like individual stocks. One is Global X China Consumer, with holdings in auto companies like Denway Motors and Dongfeng Motor Group; Home Inns & Hotel Management, with 600 hotels scattered around China; and New Oriental Education & Technology, China's largest provider of private education services, including test preparation and online learning, founded in 1993. The Global X fund carries an expense ratio that's relatively low, at 0.7 percent. Claymore/Alphashares China Small Cap has the same expense ratio, along with many of the same holdings, plus some intriguing ADRs like Ctrip International (CTRP), packaged travel, and NetEase.com (NTES), provider of online Chinese-language services, including games.

The Chinese economy has grown fourteenfold in the past three decades, with 2010 marking the sixteenth straight year of increased output. China's GDP became the world's second-largest in 2010, and there are predictions that it will overtake American GDP in the next twenty years. My favorite China mutual fund is Matthews China, which has extremely low turnover (5 percent, according to Morningstar, meaning that it holds the average stock for well over a decade), a sign that its managers are confident in their choices (mostly domestic) for the long haul. The fund's returns have been volatile, rising 65 percent in 2006 and 70 percent in 2007 but then losing 49 percent in 2008 before bouncing back by 78 percent in 2009. It's a wild ride, and you just have to hang on. Overall, the fund has returned an average of 20 percent annually for the ten years ending early December 2010. The stock pickers at Matthews specialize in Asia, and their India fund is another excellent choice—similarly volatile but highly productive.

This is a good time for a word about volatility. The Margin of Safety strategy strives for low volatility for the portfolio as a whole—even though individual holdings of stocks, bonds, or currency might fluctuate. In fact, one of the advantages of our strategy is that it *enables* you to own assets, like aspiring-markets domestic stocks, that can bounce up and down sharply because you also own much calmer bonds, as well as hedges that move in the opposite direction from stocks.

It's no wonder that investors in 2009 put an additional

$75 billion into emerging markets equity funds—a figure that almost precisely matches the *outflow* from developed-market funds, according to Standard & Poor's. There is, of course, a risk that the timing isn't perfect for investing in such funds. With other investors moving to emerging markets, prices could be inflated. But don't wait for shares to drop. They may not. And market timing, as I warn in Chapter 5, is never a good idea. Over the longer term, by which I mean the five years required for *all* stock investing, aspiring economies are the place for at least one-fifth of your equity assets.

SMALL COMPANIES, BIG GAINS

In 1981, an economist named Rolf Banz, fresh from earning his PhD at the University of Chicago, documented a fact of financial life that translates to profits today in the Margin of Safety strategy. Banz discovered the "small-firm effect," which can be defined very simply: *The smaller the stock's market capitalization, the larger the return.* If you break down stocks into ten groups, or deciles, according to their market cap, then the stocks in the first decile—the largest of the large-caps—return the least and the stocks in the tenth decile—the smallest of the small—return the most, and there's a fairly steady progression in between. According to Morningstar data, first-decile stocks returned 9.1 percent annually, on average, between 1926 and 2009 while fifth-decile stocks returned 11.3 percent and tenth-decile stocks, 13.1 percent.

The bottom two deciles, with stocks below $500 million in market capitalization, are typically considered "micro-cap" stocks. O'Shaughnessy, in *What Works on Wall Street,* found that between 1952 and 2003, returns for stocks with market caps between $100 million and $250 million produced average annual returns that were 3.3 percentage points greater than stocks with market caps above $1 billion. The reason: Micro-caps are, he wrote, "least efficiently priced." Knowledge about the companies is lacking because, for one thing, so few analysts cover them. For instance, Stryker, a medical device company with a $21 billion market cap, is covered by twenty-eight professional stock analysts, according to Yahoo! Finance, but Atrion, which is in the same business but has a market cap of $300 million, is covered by just one.

Besides inefficiency, micro-caps have another advantage over mega-cap stocks: They can grow spectacularly in size. With sales of $700 million, it's possible that sales of micro-cap retailer Hot Topic could grow by a factor of 10, or even 100. But if Walmart's sales increased by a factor of 40, it would account for all of the sales of goods and services in the United States.

With micro-caps, the higher returns come with a price that you might expect: increased volatility. While the standard deviation of large-caps is about 20 percent annually, that of micro-caps is 33 percent. The best one-year performance for small-caps was a gain of 143 percent; the worst was a loss of 58 percent. That's a range of 201 percentage points! By contrast, the range between best year and worst year for large-caps was 97 points. Over five-year periods, the average annual difference between best and worst was 73 points for micro-caps and 41 for large-caps.

Like aspiring-markets stocks, micro-caps will take you on a bumpy ride. Let's consider a double dose: a micro-cap in an aspiring market—in this case, Macao, a former Portuguese colony that is now part of the People's Republic of China but enjoys a special status, similar to Hong Kong. The company is Deswell Industries, which makes plastic parts for electronic devices and assembles such products as telephones and radar detectors. Deswell shares, which trade in the United States on the NASDAQ (so you can buy them as easily as you can Microsoft), are owned by such respected institutions as Fidelity Low-Priced Stock Mutual Fund and Royce Micro-Cap Trust, a closed-end fund that trades on the New York Stock Exchange.

In December 2010, Deswell had a market capitalization of just $57 million, almost a *sub*-micro-cap. Profits were not impressive, but they existed. Sales had fallen, but the balance sheet was strong: $41 million in cash and short-term investments at latest report and no debt at all. Several of Deswell's measures of valuation were extremely attractive: a price-to-book ratio of 0.5 (in other words, you're buying the company for half its net worth on the balance sheet) and a price-to-sales ratio of 0.7. Deswell is certainly risky, but it appears to be a speculative stock that could pay off.

Here's another example: United Online, one of the top holdings of Wasatch Micro-Cap Value, a mutual fund with a strong record. United, with a market cap of $579 million, has three businesses, all online: flower marketing, social networking for classmates, and e-mail services (NetZero) for people who dial up access to the Internet. In December 2010, the stock was trading at a forward P/E of 7, based on expected earnings for the full year. Its P/S ratio was just 0.6 and price-to-cash flow just 3.8. United had another enticingly low ratio: its PEG, or P/E divided by its predicted average annual earnings growth for the next five years. United's PEG was around 1.0, often a sign of a bargain. United has $330 million in debt, but it also has more than $100 million in cash in the bank, plus a copious flow of cash from its operations: $167 million in 2009. United even pays a dividend of 40 cents, for a yield of 5.9 percent. Again, this is a risky stock—but the risk seems to have been taken into account in its low price.

Among money managers specializing in small-cap value stocks, few have better track records than Jay Weinstein, who runs the Bethesda, Maryland, firm Oak Forest Investment Management. Every year, for my column in *Kiplinger's Personal Finance* magazine, I pick ten top stocks for the next twelve months, drawing on the selections of analysts I admire. Weinstein's choice often finishes on top—as it did in 2008—and his picks for 2005 through 2007 averaged gains of 55 percent. In recent years (2008–2010), Weinstein has come back to a *single* stock: Atrion, which makes sophisticated devices used in heart and eye surgery, among other surgical procedures. Atrion's stock price more than doubled in the five years ending October 2010, but it remains the quintessential overlooked, risky, and potentially explosive (in the best way) tiny company.

Sales and net income have risen every year since 2002. The company has a gorgeous balance sheet, with no debt, and its valuations—while not nearly as attractive as Deswell's—are, nonetheless, remarkably low for a firm growing quickly in a high-tech sector. For instance, Atrion's forward P/E ratio is 14, well below the industry average. As I write, Atrion's earnings rose 16 percent and sales 7 percent in the most recent quarter of a generally dismal year for the economy.

Deswell, United Online, and Atrion are very, very small. Combined, their market caps represent about one-third of 1 percent of the value of ExxonMobil. For that reason, they can be volatile—investors buying or selling large amounts of stock can push prices sharply up or down. But each holds the potential for big gains. The other risk for a micro-cap stock is that it might be swept away in a competitive tide and disappear entirely. Diversification is essential, but choices among good mutual funds are limited. Many funds that profess to own micro-caps actually own many stocks with market caps above $500 million. And the incentive to start a micro-cap fund is low, since a well-run fund that specializes in small stocks has to restrict its size; otherwise, if it has to make large purchases and sales, it will boost or depress the prices of the stocks it trades each time it enters the market.

My favorite among the funds is tiny Aegis Value, which focuses on micro-caps that are value stocks. Returns for the ten years ending mid-October 2010 have exceeded the S&P 500 by an incredible average of ten percentage points annually. Among the fund's top holdings are Delta Apparel, a sportswear manufacturer with a market cap of just $128 million and a P/S ratio of 0.3, and BofI Holding, an Internet bank with a cap of $126 million and a forward P/E of 6. The average Aegis stock has a market cap of $229 million. The disadvantage is that, like most micro-cap funds, this one carries a high expense ratio (1.5 percent), justified by the fact that ferreting out the condition of an obscure and miniature company is more labor-intensive than analyzing a well-known larger one.

A close second among micro-cap funds is Bridgeway Ultra-Small Company Market, which uses a proprietary quantitative system (rather than active human management) to pick stocks and, for that reason, carries an expense ratio of just 0.75 percent. Like Aegis, the Bridgeway fund has thoroughly whipped both the S&P 500 and the Russell and Lipper micro-cap indexes over the past ten years. The fund's average stock has a market cap of just $158 million and among the top holdings is Tessco Technologies, which provides services to big wireless users. Tessco has a cap of a mere $112 million, a forward P/E of 11, and a P/S of 0.2. Bridgeway is not all high-tech. It also owns shares of Standard Parking, which manages lots with more than one million spaces around the country, and Callon Petroleum, a tiny oil and gas exploration and production company.

Margin of Safety stock categories certainly offer variety: from solid dividend payers to more exciting developing-market, value, and micro-cap stocks. Each has its place. But, as we will see in the next chapter, stocks aren't everything.

4

WHAT TO DO: BONDS AND MORE

In the Margin of Safety strategy, bonds are just as important as stocks, and hedges and currencies are absolutely critical. In this chapter, we'll delve more deeply into the assets in your portfolio that aren't equities.

THE 5 PERCENT SOLUTION

Begin with the bond. A bond is a contract. On one side, you the investor are the lender, turning over cash to a government agency or a business. On the other side, the borrower promises to repay you on a specific date and to provide interest along the way. While the word *bond* connotes trust or confidence, the truth is that sometimes borrowers don't live up to the bargain they've struck. Governments like Russia and Argentina and businesses like General Motors and Enron default.

Still, over the short and medium term (up to ten years),

bonds are less risky than stocks—that is, less apt to fall sharply (or even go to zero). Also, bonds lack correlation with stocks—a hedge against the bulk of your assets taking a dive at the same time. For instance, for the five years ending in 1958, large-cap stocks returned an average of 22 percent annually while long-term U.S. Treasury bonds returned 0.2 percent. For the five years ending in 2004, stocks lost an average of 2.3 percent annually but T-bonds scored positive returns of 10.3 percent. In the debacle of 2008, when the S&P 500 lost three-eighths of its value, the Vanguard Long-Term U.S. Treasury mutual fund *gained* nearly one-fourth. In a period when investors are especially averse to risks, bonds offer a safe harbor, and we will probably see the value of Treasury bonds rise when stocks next take a big fall.

With moderate inflation of less than 3 percent a year, your goal should be a 5 percent return from bonds—the "5 Percent Solution"—and the easiest way to get it is to buy debt and hold it to maturity. Trading bonds frequently is confusing, expensive, and unnecessary. Instead, build a ladder with your bonds. For example, you might own ten separate $10,000 bonds, maturing in succession, with maturities spaced out every year. Say you begin in 2011 and have bonds that mature annually from 2012 to 2021. When the first bond matures in 2012, take the $10,000 you receive and invest in a new bond that matures in 2022. If rates rise in the meantime, you will be getting more interest than with your bond maturing in 2011. If rates fall, the bonds you already own will be earning more than today's bonds—a good feeling.

What is trickier is the question of which bonds to buy. Since a bond is an IOU, the key question is whether you are going to get your money back.

Throughout modern history, the United States has been viewed by lenders as a dependable borrower. Lately, however, as the total debt of the Treasury rises to record levels, you hear talk of a possible default by the U.S. government. It's never happened, but the prospect is not entirely out of the realm of conventional risk measurement. You can actually buy credit default swaps—essentially, insurance policies—against the possibility that the U.S. Treasury won't pay interest and principal on its bonds. At the start of 2008, the cost was tiny: just 8 basis points, or 0.08 percent—$8 a year to insure against the default of $10,000 in T-bonds for five years. But by February 2009, that cost had jumped to 100 basis points before settling back, by midyear, to about 40, where it remained late in 2010. Among major industrial nations, Germany at the time was slightly less risky than the United States, China's rate was 56 basis points, and Spain's was 196.

Of course, an intriguing question is whether you can trust the seller, or counterparty to the swaps—that is, the institution that is insuring you against a default by the U.S. government. It's the same question that buyers of insurance against defaults of subprime mortgages neglected to ask—until too late. Still, I am not advising you to buy the credit insurance—only that you use it as a guide to risk. By definition, *nothing* is free of Knightian uncertainty, but Treasuries provide the best safety net.

There remain two problems, however. The first is that there's no telling when inflation will rear its ugly head. Although the Consumer Price Index has been tame in recent years, financial history is filled with examples of nations that, deliberately or not, inflated their way out of debt. In the U.S. case, that would mean repaying interest and principal on bonds with cheaper and cheaper dollars—that is, dollars that have declined in their power to purchase goods and services because prices have risen.

TIPS FOR INFLATION PROTECTION

This problem has an elegantly simple solution: Treasury Inflation-Protected Securities, or TIPS. When you buy TIPS, you make a loan that carries a promise of repayment that's adjusted to the annual increase in the Consumer Price Index. The easiest way to think about the inflation bonus is that it increases your annual rate of interest. For example, a recently issued TIPS bond, maturing in ten years, carried a coupon indicating a real interest rate of 1.25 percent. If inflation runs 3 percent (the average for the past century), you will collect interest of 4.25 percent (1.25 percent guaranteed, plus the inflation premium) over the life of the bond.

TIPS were launched by the Clinton administration in 1997, but economists of varying ideological persuasions had been advocating them for years. The late conservative Nobel laureate Milton Friedman wrote in 1971 that TIPS would put an end to the "disgraceful shell game" by which the government borrowed from investors and repaid them in dollars whose value was eroded by inflation that the government itself created. Further to the left, Nobel laureate James Tobin argued that TIPS would help "savers of limited means and knowledge, [who] should not be forced to gamble either on the price level or on the stock market."

If you hold your TIPS to maturity—and if the United States does not default or manipulate the Consumer Price Index (as, for example, Argentina has been accused of doing)—then the securities carry no credit or interest-rate risk. But if you need to sell your bonds before maturity, you may not get what you paid for them. The reason is that the market for an individual issue of TIPS can be fairly illiquid, and demand from investors can rise and fall for all sorts of reasons—including investment fashion. For instance, if inflation has been low for a long time and stocks are attractive, investors might abandon TIPS for securities that hold out the prospect of much higher returns. That would cause the price of TIPS to fall.

With a plain-vanilla bond (that is, a Treasury bond without the inflation bonus), investors are also subject to such whims, but, more important, they risk the vagaries of interest rates, driven by inflation expectations. With inflation forecast at 2 percent, a ten-year T-bond yielding 5 percent looks very attractive, but if inflation rises a bit and people see even more on the horizon, then investors will demand yields of 6 percent, 7 percent, or more, and your 5 percent bond won't attract any buyers if you try to sell it for what you paid originally. Its price drops, and, if you have to sell, you're a loser. Even if you hold it to maturity, your opportunity cost is high—that is, you have forgone the higher interest payments you could have collected. No one can predict the direction of interest rates, but laddering protects you against a persistent rise in inflation, since each year you will be trading lower-yielding bonds for higher-yielding.

The second problem with bonds is that, in scary times, Treasuries have been seen as a safe haven, so you don't make much on what you lend out. Investors around the world have been pouring their savings into America's bonds, driving down interest rates. (Every borrower wants the lowest rates, and the Treasury can say, in effect, "Since eager lenders are lining up to give us money, we'll only borrow from you at a couple of percentage points a year.")

Coping with low bond yields involves patience. Yields will rise. You can count on it. In the meantime, you can get higher interest by moving from bonds issued by the U.S. Treasury to bonds of federal agencies, state and local governments, and corporations. In the past, I didn't worry too much about small differences in interest rates. If only one-tenth of your portfolio is in bonds, there's little need to quibble about half a percent. But if bonds are half your holdings—as they should be—then tenths of a point can mean a lot.

REACHING FOR HIGHER YIELD

The financial crisis of 2008–2009 taught us that the U.S. government will stand behind debt issued by its agencies. Such loans were said to carry only an "implicit" guarantee from the Treasury. Bondholders in Fannie Mae and Freddie Mac, the giant and (as it turned out) profligate providers of funding for mortgages, were bailed out, and we can expect them to get the same treatment next time. You can buy Fannie and Freddie or choose from other agencies, like the Tennessee Valley Authority, a corporation created in 1933 and wholly owned by the federal government, that operates one of the nation's largest electric power systems.

In early December 2010, a TVA bond maturing in seven years was yielding 2.6 percent and one maturing in twenty years was yielding 4.6 percent. By comparison, standard Treasury bonds with similar maturities were yielding about four-tenths of a point more.

With all bonds, shorter maturities are safer. If rates rise, their prices fall less than the prices of longer-term bonds—so, if you have to sell before maturity, you will escape a big loss. If you do hold a bond to maturity, short-term debt gets you cash quicker, so you can reinvest it in higher-yielding bonds.

When Treasuries and agencies are hugely popular, as in 2010, to get more attractive yields in the shorter term, you have to buy corporate debt—investment-grade bonds, rated between BBB- and AAA by Standard & Poor's or between Baa3 and Aaa by Moody's (I'll use the S&P ratings here as an illustration). Regulators allow banks to keep bonds with these ratings in their portfolios, and that should be good enough for you, too—as long as your portfolio is diversified, with a bunch of bonds, not just one or two.

A JPMorgan Chase bond, rated A+ and maturing in March 2020, was yielding 4.7 percent at the same time that a Treasury with the same maturity was yielding only 3.2 percent. A Walmart bond, maturing in July 2020, was yielding 4 percent.

Bond ratings aren't guarantees, and many highly rated issues of mortgage debt securities defaulted during the recent financial crisis. As a result, ratings agencies have become more conservative. They don't want their reputations tarnished further, so their judgments are probably more trustworthy at this point.

If you are willing to endure a bit more risk, consider bonds from solid companies like Masco Corporation, a building products company whose notes maturing in six years were yielding 5.7 percent. At the same time, Kraft Foods had bonds due in ten years yielding 3.8 percent, even though their S&P rating is lower than Masco's, at BBB-. A Seagate Technology bond, rated BB+ (just below investment grade) and maturing in 2016, was yielding a juicy 6.5 percent.

Another alternative is the municipal bond, issued by a state or local agency, with interest exempt from federal (and often state and local) taxes. The average yield on a ten-year AAA-rated muni in October 2010 was 2.6 percent, the very same as for a ten-year Treasury at the time; the average twenty-year A-rated muni was yielding 4.4 percent, compared with 3.6 percent for a similarly maturing T-bond. But the interest-rate range for munis is wide and depends not just on rating but also on location and on whether a bond is a general obligation (GO) security, meaning that the full faith and credit of the state or locality stands behind it, or a debt supported by revenues from a particular project, like tolls from a turnpike or rents from a building. Because of their tax advantage, munis rarely yield significantly more than Treasuries, but worries about state local finances have made munis especially attractive lately. For instance, a muni that pays interest of 4 percent is equivalent, for someone in a 35 percent tax bracket, to a taxable bond yielding 6.2 percent. Make sure, however, that you understand the terms of the muni you are buying. For example, many long-term munis are callable—meaning that at a certain point, perhaps ten or fifteen years before maturity, an issuer can take advantage of declining interest rates by paying off the bonds and issuing new ones, much as a homeowner can refinance. Munis, of course, make no sense for tax-deferred or tax-free portfolios like IRAs and 401(k) plans.

My preference is for individual bonds, bought through a broker or bank, or, in the case of Treasuries, directly through the TreasuryDirect site on the Internet. With individual bonds, you get what you really want, and you can wait for maturity and reinvest the cash. Mutual funds own an array of bonds, maturing at different times, and managers usually have broad discretion to buy and sell based on their forecasts of interest rates. If you own individual bonds with an average yield of 5 percent, you can be assured (barring defaults) that you'll make a 5 percent return for the year ahead. But if you own a bond mutual fund, anything can happen. If rates are falling, the manager may decide to take profits and sell bonds whose prices have risen. If they are rising, the opposite might occur, and the 5 percent gain you were expecting turns into a 5 percent loss.

Still, mutual funds are fine if managers are tightly constrained (so you know what you are buying) and if fees are low. Ideal is an exchange-traded fund like PIMCO 3–7 Year U.S. Treasury Index, with an expense ratio of just 0.15 percent. In late 2010, the fund owned twenty-one separate T-note issues, with maturities ranging from 2013 to 2017. In 2011, management will probably sell its 2013 notes and buy 2018 ones to replace them.

Bonds are hedges against the uncertainties of the stock

part of your portfolio. Well-chosen and held to maturity, they will provide a steady stream of income. With stocks, you can gain 25 percent in a great year or lose 25 percent in a terrible one, but with bonds, you'll putter along with a 5 percent solution, which narrows a $100,000 portfolio's loss from $25,000 to $10,000 with a 50/50 split between stocks and bonds. That's what we want, but there's even more insurance at hand.

A BASKET FULL OF MONEY

A sharp decline in the value of the dollar is always a real possibility, especially with the United States importing so much more than it is exporting. However, whether conscious of that fact or not, practically all Americans are *long* the dollar—that is, betting on it to rise. For instance, our paychecks and our Social Security benefits are in dollars, as are the dividends and interest payments on most of our investments. To gain exposure to other currencies, we can buy foreign stocks, as I recommended in Chapter 3, or buy shares of U.S.-based companies that do most of their business abroad. For example, 65 percent of the sales and 53 percent of the profits of McDonald's Corporation come from foreign operations. Coca-Cola collects 75 percent of its revenues outside North America. For Intel Corporation, 85 percent of sales are outside the United States.

But there is another way to hedge against a decline in

the dollar: You can simply buy foreign currencies. In the past, the only efficient ways for an average investor to purchase euros, yen, or Swiss francs were through the Forex (foreign exchange) or futures market. Either way, you bet directly on the direction of a foreign currency versus the dollar, and, either way, you used enormous leverage to amplify your gains (or losses). In the case of Forex, you can buy $1 million worth of euros, for instance, for $10,000. If the euro rises by 1 percent, you double your money; if it falls 1 percent, you lose your entire stake. With futures, you make similar leveraged bets on the value of a currency months or years from now.

Such currency trading is not a game for amateurs. The purpose of buying foreign currencies in the Margin of Safety strategy is to hedge—that is, to insure against disaster—not to score a trading coup. So we need a calmer method of protection. Luckily, such a method now exists—in the form of currency exchange-traded funds, or ETFs, securities that you buy and sell on major exchanges. Most ETFs own stocks, but these own foreign currencies. For instance, CurrencyShares Japanese Yen Trust, which trades on the New York Stock Exchange, puts your dollars into Japanese bank accounts, which earn infinitesimal interest, so the value of your investment rises or falls with the movement of the yen against the dollar. In 2008, its first full year, the fund returned 23 percent; in its second, it lost 3 percent. In the case of a stock fund, a few years of returns would tell us next to nothing about its manager's ability to pick equities, but a currency ETF has substantial validity from the start because its prices simply reflect the movements of one currency against another. The yen fund charges a relatively low fee of 0.4 percent. CurrencyShares, a product of the money-management firm Rydex, also has ETFs that invest in euros, Swiss francs, Australian dollars, Russian rubles, British pounds, and a few more.

Rather than buying funds that own individual currencies, you can buy a basket from WisdomTree, an ETF firm launched by hedge fund manager Michael Steinhardt and financial scholar Jeremy Siegel. For example, the Wisdom-Tree Dreyfus Emerging Currency fund invests in currencies issued by such aspiring economies as China, Brazil, South Korea, India, South Africa, Poland, Turkey, and Taiwan. The fund, launched in May 2009, rose 10 percent in its first seven months. It carries a reasonable fee of 0.55 percent. WisdomTree offers individual currency ETFs as well, for countries ranging from Japan to Brazil to New Zealand.

Or you can take a more direct approach by simply buying debt of other countries, with interest and principal rendered in those nations' own currencies. In December 2010, for instance, two-year notes denominated in Australian dollars were yielding 5.1 percent interest (more than four points more than similar U.S.-dollar notes); ten-year Australian bonds were yielding 5.6 percent (2.4 points more than American bonds). The interest payments themselves are attractive, especially at the lower end of the maturity scale, for currencies like the Canadian dollar and the Swedish kroner. But if it is a hedge alone that you want, then consider Swiss debt—ten-year bonds were yielding a minuscule 1.7 percent, but Switzerland's economic management has been superbly stable.

Not even Switzerland, however, is immune to Knightian uncertainty—which, by definition, is all about surprise of the most unpleasant and shocking kind. Nothing can protect you completely from what you can neither know nor imagine. My objective here is to soften the blow, and the most powerful mitigation comes from a hedge of the sort I introduced in Chapter 2: the bear fund that, using derivatives, rises when the market falls. There are other derivative hedges to choose from as well. Here are three of them.

BUYING PUTS

A *put* option is a contract that gives you the right to sell a security at a set price during a set period. Say you believe that a stock called Al's Turbines is headed for trouble. Assume that in January 2011, you could buy an option giving you the right to "put"—or force someone else to purchase—Al's at $10 per share in January 2013. The price of the put was about 60 cents. At the time of your purchase, Al's was trading at roughly $17 a share. Let's say you purchase puts on 10,000 shares at a total cost of $6,000.

Let's also say that over two years, Al's drops to just $7. You exercise your option, which lets you sell Al's to another investor for $10. You go into the market and buy 10,000 shares of Al's at $7, immediately sell it at $10, and you receive $30,000 ($3 x 10,000 shares), minus your original $6,000 put investment, for a profit of $24,000.

All you really need to know about puts, which you buy through a broker, like stocks, is that they make money when prices fall. You can accept different degrees of risk. In the example above, if Al's drops from $17 to $11 after two years, your puts will finish out of the money—that is, above $10—and expire worthless. In this case, however, you would have profited if you had bought puts with a strike price of $15—but they would cost more (say, $2 each, in this case) to start with. Also remember that you don't have to wait until maturity to sell your puts. If Al's is headed down fast, then the value of your put will rise and you can sell at a profit even before it gets in the money.

You can also buy puts that amount to hedges on the broad market. A wide variety of S&P 500 puts are for sale, including some that protect you against a major decline. Assume that in March 2011, you could buy a put letting you sell SPDRs (or Spiders, shares that are linked to the S&P 500 Index and trading at one-tenth of that index's value) at $97 in September. At the time, assume SPDRs were trading at $115, so you make a profit if the index falls 16 percent in six months. The cost of puts on 10,000 shares was $19,000.

If the S&P should crash by 25 percent—down to about 862 from 1150, your proceeds from each put would be about $11 ($97 minus $86), or $110,000 for your 10,000 shares. Subtract your cost of $19,000, and you have made a profit of around $90,000—perhaps enough to cushion the fall in the stocks you hold in the rest of your portfolio.

A put is much closer to a conventional insurance premium. In the S&P case, you pay $19,000 for six months of coverage, no matter what the market does. You get your reward if the market tanks—and the more it falls, the more you get.

The protection that I just described—against a market drop of around 15 percent over half a year—makes sense for about $500,000 worth of stock assets. The cost of protection is not cheap, but say the market drops 30 percent. Your losses without put insurance are $150,000. But with the insurance I laid out, the losses drop to a few thousand dollars. (Here is the full calculation: 30 percent decline in S&P from 1150 equals 805, equivalent to SPDR price of $80.50. Subtract $80.50 from $97 and get $16.50. Multiply by 10,000 puts and get $165,000. Subtract initial cost of puts: $165,000 minus $19,000 equals $146,000.)

The options market is tough to understand, and prices are determined not only by the depth of the decline you are insuring against, but also by the current environment for volatility. For most investors, bear funds are a lot easier to master, but at times when few people are expecting a decline, puts can be a bargain.

Also, consider buying individual stock puts on companies whose decline would almost certainly correlate with that of the market as a whole—or exceed it. A good example is Citigroup. Assume that in March 2011, the stock is trading at $3.50 a share, and you could buy a put with a strike price of $2.50 in January 2013 for 37 cents. A hedge of 10,000 Citigroup puts would cost $3,700. Let's assume that Citi goes bankrupt, the government takes over, and the stock drops to a few pennies a share. You'll make about $20,000 ($25,000 minus a few cents times 10,000 puts minus the $3,700 initial cost). This is the ultimate insurance policy against a meltdown, and the price is certainly right.

PUTTING ON A COLLAR

You can think of a hedge as a backstop or as a *collar*—a financial term that indicates limits on both the upside and the downside of an investment. As the new millennium began, one of the most popular and accessible collars was the principal-protected note, which came in abundant varieties. The best-known were MITTS, or Market Index Target-Term Securities, issued by Merrill Lynch. Other varieties were issued by Lehman Brothers and other firms.

They worked like this: You bought a five-year bond and, instead of being paid a fixed rate of interest, you received the increase (or partial increase) in a particular stock index, such as the S&P 500 or the Nikkei 225. If the index fell over the five years, you still got your principal back. In other words, this collar limits your downside to zero and gives you an upside that, in some cases, amounted to the entire rise in an index. Too good to be true? Not exactly. First of all, in 2000, when these securities became popular, the S&P had not suffered a five-year loss since the mid-1970s and had only declined twice over such a period since 1941. Second, Merrill and the other firms pocketed the S&P dividends. Third, they had the use of your money for five years.

Still, as a hedge, principal-protected notes made good sense. Many of them were traded on the American and New York Stock Exchange, with decent liquidity, and, as insurance policies, they were relatively cheap. The only problem was that these securities were debt, and the borrower was the investment firm that issued them, as purchasers of the Lehman notes learned to their chagrin after Lehman went bankrupt.

Principal-protected notes (also called supertrack notes) almost completely disappeared after 2008; a few years later they began to resurface—but with quite a few wrinkles. For instance, in early 2010 Citigroup issued notes maturing in 2015 that were linked to gains in the S&P, but only up to a cap of 55 percent (or roughly 10 percent annually, on average). Barclays offered notes that gave you double the returns of an energy-stock index, but with a limit of 21 percent and protection on the downside only up to a 15 percent loss; after that, you lost money on a one-for-one basis, so a decline of 25 percent meant you would lose 10 percent.

In gun-shy times, with investment firms so risk-averse, principal-protected notes are not very attractive, but keep an eye on them for the future. Just beware of complexity. Make sure you understand what you're buying, and who stands behind it.

SELLING COVERED CALLS

Here's a less complicated collar that uses derivatives. An option is a right to buy or sell something at a fixed price over a fixed period. You can ask your broker to write an option on stocks you own—a process also termed selling covered calls (*covered* because you actually own the stock to start with).

Here's how it works: Assume you own 1,000 shares of Acme Microchips. The stock is trading at $40 a share, and there is an active market in options expiring in January 2013 at $50 a share. The price for such an option, a little less than two years from the date of expiration, is $7 a share. So you could sell 1,000 covered calls to another investor for $7,000. If Acme rises from $40 to $70, the buyer will exercise his options and pocket the $20 difference between $70 and $50, times 1,000 shares. That's $20,000 minus $7,000, for a profit of $13,000.

But look at it from your own point of view. You receive $7,000 in return for the options. No matter what happens, you keep that money—a return of 17.5 percent over two years, or nearly 9 percent annually on your Acme investment. If the stock rises to $50—a 25 percent gain—the options won't be exercised. Above that, they will, so you sacrifice the upside. If Acme doubles or triples in value, you will be kicking yourself.

What if, on the other hand, Acme falls? The value of your portfolio will decline, of course, but you'll still have your $7,000. If Acme drops by 25 percent, to $30 a share, your loss without the calls would have been $10,000, but, with the calls, it is reduced to $3,000. If Acme rises 25 percent, to $50, your gain will be $17,000. If it rises 100 percent, your gain is still $17,000—rather than the $40,000 you would have had without the calls.

Selling covered calls is a way to get cash in your pocket and a way to limit your losses in return for limiting your profits. Just as with puts, you can buy or sell calls on indexes as well as individual stocks.

You can create your own collars more directly by instructing your broker to sell index funds or stocks when they reach specific prices. In the Acme example above, you could create a sell order at $50 and at $36. When the stock increases 25 percent or declines 10 percent, you're out of it.

The advantage of covered calls over the sell-order strategy is that, with the calls, you get paid while you wait.

Also, when you order a sale on a stock's or an index fund's decline, you run the risk of being whipsawed. Acme could hit $36 on Tuesday and get sold; on Wednesday, it may jump to $45. Plus, a swift, sharp decline could blow right past your floor.

In the Margin of Safety strategy, the nonstocks are as important as the stocks. Even more important than both is the *approach* you take to investing—the strategy, tactics, and style. That's what we will examine next, in the form of a brand-new rulebook for investors.

5

THE NEW RULEBOOK

The mission of the New Rulebook is to combine high returns with a high degree of security. Of course, you can't maximize two variables at the same time. But, as shown in this book, there are ways to make a productive trade: slightly lower returns than the historic averages for considerably less risk. That balance is what most investors want and need, and it's what the Margin of Safety strategy provides.

I'll begin with five broad principles, then move to eighteen specific rules ...

THE FIVE PRINCIPLES

1. IT'S UP TO YOU

Investing is a distinctly human endeavor. There are vast choices, and, even with a strategy like the Margin of Safety as a guide, your own decisions will ultimately determine your success. It is no easy matter to change your instincts or your personality so that you are more investing-friendly, but the first persistent fact to recognize about investing is that, with the wrong attitude, you cannot win.

The Margin of Safety strategy provides a backstop, a buffer, a safety net to protect you against both the vagaries of the market and the mistakes you will inevitably make. But no strategy can do it all. You need to understand who you are and turn yourself into a better investor.

Begin by recognizing that successful investing is an act of faith. You are entrusting your money to someone else—a mutual fund, a business, the U.S. Treasury—and, once you have made your choice, you need the confidence and the patience to stick with it. Disrupt your long-term plan with spur-of-the-moment selling (or spur-of-the-moment buying) only in the rare instance that something has *changed* (a value stock has become a growth stock, a key product has failed, or new competitors have joined the market)—not in the general atmosphere but within the investment itself.

Ben Graham wrote in *The Intelligent Investor* that "the investor's chief problem—and even his worst enemy—is himself." Investing requires the virtues of moderation: a clear head, a calm attitude. But, because it involves money, investing is also an endeavor that generates hot emotions—and not a few of the temptations of at least some of the Seven Deadly Sins, especially greed, envy, and vanity. The demands of investing naturally push us to act against our own best interests.

In the face of such powerful forces, what can an investor do? One practical answer is to adopt a *productive self-conception*—a useful way of looking at yourself, at who you are, from the outside. Graham taught that investors should think of themselves as partners in great businesses (or, in the case of bonds, as lenders to sound borrowers). Stocks are not numbers on a page; they are shares—literally—of companies that are engaged in real-life activities. Join these businesses. Be a proud owner.

Many years ago, I wrote about the distinction between two kinds of investors—Outsmarters and Partakers. Outsmarters believe they are clever enough to see what others can't, that they can beat the system with brilliant stock picks, timely short sales, or a move into cash at just the right moment. Partakers, on the other hand, believe that they can profit from participating in the growth of the American—and, more and more, the global—economy. They see the stock market as a gift. It allows them to become partners in great businesses, like P&G and Exxon-Mobil and Apple. Outsmarting rarely works. Partaking has a rich and profitable history.

In the three decades I have written a financial column, I have concluded that most investors can't tolerate the fear generated by a bear market. They can't just stand there; they have to do something. Often, that's a mistake. But, if you know yourself, you will find ways to counteract the desire to act. The overall portfolio structure that the Margin of Safety strategy recommends is one antidote. There are others, such as not looking at your portfolio online every day or even every week and not paying the slightest attention to short-term predictions about the market or the economy.

Also understand that no investor has it easy all the time. Bear markets happen, stocks never go straight up, and all your investments won't make money. Warren Buffett once invested heavily in USAir, even though he fully understood the dangers of airline stocks—which his mentor Graham had warned against back in 1947. Buffett paid the price for giving in to his temptation and later said about the industry: "You've got huge fixed costs, you've got strong labor unions, and you've got commodity pricing. That is not a great recipe for success. I have an 800 number now that I call if I get the urge to buy an airline stock. I call at 2 in the morning and I say: 'My name is Warren, and I'm an aeroholic.' And then they talk me down."

A successful investor owns up to his mistakes and learns from them. I guess I am as good an example as any. In the 1999 book I coauthored, *Dow 36,000*, I offered a vigorously optimistic view of stock investing. I was wrong on a prediction that the equity premium—that is, the higher returns that stocks achieve compared to bonds— would wither away as investors grew more confident in equities. Under such circumstances, I believed, the Dow would rise to a new plateau and future returns would fall. It didn't happen. What have I learned in the meantime? First, the world can change. Those changes are at the root of the Margin of Safety investment strategy. Second, the efficiency of markets should never be underestimated. That big equity risk premium, which seemed to defy history and logic, turned out to be based on fears that turned out to be justified.

2. MARKETS ARE EFFICIENT, BUT . . .

Yes, markets are efficient. Not always and everywhere, but the vast majority of the time. This idea is both comforting and anxiety-producing. Let me explain.

Under the Efficient Market Hypothesis, or EMH, the price of a stock is determined by everything that could possibly be known about it, including profits that are anticipated in the future.

The reason this concept, introduced in Chapter 3, is important is that you, as an investor, don't need to spend your time gathering all the details about a company's finances, its position in an industry, or its customers. That knowledge, gathered by others, has determined today's price. As Graham wrote: "In the area of near-term selectivity, the current year's results of the company are generally common property in Wall Street; next year's results, to the extent that they are predictable, are already being carefully considered."

You can assume that today's price is correct—in the sense that it is the serious opinion of thousands, or even millions, of investors around the world. If you believe in the company and want to become a partner, then any time is the right time to buy the stock because, chances are, the price today reflects what the company is really worth.

Market timing—that is, trying to guess where the market (or an individual stock) will go next—is a fool's errand. "Illusions of Patterns and Patterns of Illusions" is what Leonard Mlodinow titles one of the chapters of his book *The Drunkard's Walk.* In 200 tosses of a coin, he writes, "it is easy to find patterns in the data"—like four heads in a row, followed by four tails. When I walk through a Las Vegas casino, I often see long runs of black or red recorded on the scoreboard of a roulette table—once I noticed ten blacks in a row. What is the significance of these patterns? Nothing at all. The next roll of the little roulette ball has a 50/50 chance of coming up red. We are hardwired to believe in patterns and to distrust or ignore randomness, but it is the dynamic behind the workings of the stock market. As Burton Malkiel puts it, the market's "future steps or directions cannot be predicted on the basis of past actions"—neither on the basis of fundamental analysis (looking at the economics of a nation or a business) nor on the basis of technical analysis (looking at the movement of data points, such as stock prices, on a chart). This is the reality behind the quotation from Peter L. Bernstein that begins this book: Conceding that you don't know the future is the beginning of investment wisdom.

Yet it is prediction, rather than explanation, that preoccupies the financial media. In my book *The Secret Code of the Superior Investor,* I told readers, "Don't watch CNBC in broad daylight." Smart and engaging broadcasters push a relentless theme: The person we are interviewing will magically predict the future. But the truthful answer to the question of what's going to happen next is, as Lord Keynes said in Chapter 2, "We simply do not know!"

So, as an investor, you are liberated. You don't have to spend your time trying to divine the short-term movement of markets and stocks because that movement can't be predicted any better by you than by anyone else. Because of the EMH, Malkiel wrote that "a blindfolded chimpanzee throwing darts at the *Wall Street Journal* could select a portfolio that would do as well as the experts." What we can say about the future, however, is that, if it is somewhat like the past, then over the long term stocks, as a whole, will go up because human imagination keeps improving efficiency and the population keeps growing.

That's the comfort of the EMH. The anxious part is that, as an investor, you are always struggling for an edge. I am not talking here about being an Outsmarter—a self-styled genius who bets on black because she thinks the roulette wheel is slightly tilted. I am simply talking about someone who wants her stock portfolio to return

13 percent over the next ten years instead of 10 percent, or someone who worries that a Verizon bond may be riskier than AT&T bond.

If you believe in the EMH, then you will gain an edge only if you find companies that the market has somehow overlooked or doesn't fully understand. Such companies, priced inefficiently, can be found! As Buffett wrote in his 1988 letter to the shareholders of his company Berkshire Hathaway, Inc.: "Observing that the market was frequently efficient, they [i.e., certain economists] went on to conclude incorrectly that the market was always efficient. The difference between the propositions is night and day." Here is the lodestar of Buffett's own career.

In Chapter 3, I recommend three stock sectors that include an abundance of overlooked companies: value stocks (overlooked by definition), micro-caps (too small for stock analysts and big investors to bother with), and companies in aspiring markets (too far away and speaking strange languages).

As a nonexpert, you can even have an edge in finding great companies that experts miss. Peter Lynch, the former manager of the Fidelity Magellan Fund and one of the most successful stock pickers of all time, urges investors to act on their own local knowledge. As a dentist, you may be the first to recognize that a company has developed a terrific new drill and has a huge jump on the competition. As a shopper, you may notice that a new clothing chain at the mall is attracting hordes of teenagers. Among his best stock selections, Lynch discovered La Quinta motels because he stayed there on business and L'eggs pantyhose (now part of Hanesbrands Inc.) because his wife raved when they first appeared in the supermarket.

If it turns out that the market in dental-drill stocks is *not* inefficient—that others knew about the innovation and priced the stock correctly—then you really don't have that much to lose anyway. You bought your shares at the right price rather than at a particularly low price. Of course, stocks may be inefficiently priced in the *other* direction. Mister Market, thrilled at recent earnings, may become far too enthusiastic about the prospects of a company and price it too high. For that reason, beware of buying stocks that are well-loved but that you think should be even better-loved.

Through diversification, the Margin of Safety strategy takes into account the fact that stocks can be priced inefficiently to the upside. You'll be hurt when Citigroup loses 80 percent of its value, but you won't be devastated because it will represent no more than 1/100th of your holdings. The true comfort is that if you construct your portfolio as I am advising, you will have the luxury and the joy of making bets on companies you think the market has overlooked and on a future that few others recognize.

Finally, the power of the EMH should make all investors skeptical of the professed expertise of fund managers. Consider Bill Miller, who runs the Legg Mason Value fund. His extraordinary achievement was to beat the S&P 500 for fifteen years in a row—sometimes by as little as a few tenths of a percentage point, sometimes by fifteen points. But each and every year from 1991 to 2005.

In his book, *Fooled by Randomness,* Nassim Nicholas Taleb, writes, "If one puts an infinite number of monkeys in front of (strongly built) typewriters and lets them clap away, there is a certainty that one of them [will] come out with an exact version of the 'Iliad.'" The monkey typist story is an old one, and the key word here is *infinite*. But Taleb takes this hoary tale a step further. "Now that we have found that hero among monkeys, would any reader invest his life's savings on a bet that the monkey would write the 'Odyssey' next?" As it turned out, Bill Miller was no Homer. Instead, he trailed the S&P 500 badly in 2006, 2007, and 2008 and, as a result, he finished the ten years ending October 2010 behind 93 percent of his mutual-fund peers.

Past performance, as the disclaimers say, is no guarantee of future success. Thus, the case for index funds, which pick stocks by computer algorithm and charge low fees. Over the past fifteen years, Fidelity's fund that tracks the S&P 500 Index,* beat 63 percent of funds in its category (large-cap blend), mainly because it charges annual

---

* The fund is Fidelity Spartan Index, and it requires a minimum investment of $10,000. The more popular Vanguard Index 500, which also tracks the S&P benchmark large-cap index, has a smaller minimum, at $3,000, but its fee is 0.18 percent annually.

expenses of just 0.1 percent while managed funds charge about a full percentage point.

Still, searching for someone with a hot hand makes sense, which is why I cite people like fund manager Donald Yacktman in this book. If their records are merely meaningless patterns discerned in randomness, then, no harm done; chances are, these managers will do just as well as their peers. And if their records are not, you may be a winner.

3. DIVERSIFY, PLEASE

Most of the investing disasters of the past few years—the Enron scandal, the Madoff scandal, the tech bubble, the housing bubble—had something in common. The people who were badly hurt lacked the protection of diversification. Enron, for example, offered a typical 401(k): Employees could invest up to 6 percent of their base pay in a wide range of investments, including stock mutual funds like Fidelity Magellan, bonds, money-market funds, and a self-directed Schwab account that could buy practically anything. They could also choose Enron stock, purchased at the regular market price. If they bought the stock, then whatever employees contributed with their own money, the company matched, up to 50 percent, with more Enron stock. That was quite an enticement—especially since most Enron employees believed fervently in their company. When Enron went bankrupt, the average worker had three-fifths of his 401(k) invested in Enron stock. For an investor in an S&P 500 index fund, the vaporization of Enron was insignificant, since the company represented only about 1 percent of the index's assets. For an Enron employee (who also lost his job), it was a catastrophe.

Similarly, many investors with Madoff, including the Elie Wiesel Foundation for Humanity, lost nearly everything because they gave Bernie nearly everything they had. Few investors could have figured out that Madoff's history of strong returns was a scam, but all investors should have known that putting most of their eggs in a single basket was far too risky.

Tech stocks rose so fast in the 1990s that they suddenly represented a huge chunk of even a prudent investor's portfolio. Oracle jumped by a factor of fifteen between 1998 and early 2000, and eBay and Expedia each rose more than twentyfold. It was not unusual for investors on January 1, 2000, to have 90 percent of a 401(k) plan in tech stocks—which quickly fell back to earth. Even as solid a company as Intel, with its near-monopoly in the chips that account for a computer's central processing unit, lost four-fifths of its value and, for the past decade, has never come close to its 2000 peak.

Warren Buffett likes to quote Mae West as saying that "too much of a good thing can be wonderful"—meaning that if you really love a company, you can't own too much of its stock. For those of us who lack the genius and the record of a Buffett (as well as the time to become professional stock pickers), diversification is a necessity.

An individual stock may be extremely risky. If, in July 2008, you had put $20,000 into AIG, considered one of the most stable and profitable financial institutions in the world, your shares would have been worth $100 eight months later. Could you have figured out what would go wrong with AIG or with Enron, or with Lehman Brothers, for that matter? I doubt it. Sometimes, stocks go to zero, but never do all stocks go to zero at the same time. For that reason, you need to own a wide range of stocks and bonds.

How many? In 2000, economist John Y. Campbell of Harvard concluded that, for your portfolio to achieve roughly the same volatility as the market as a whole, you need to own about fifty stocks, spread out among different sectors.* How to achieve balance among sectors? Look at the way the assets of the S&P 500 (which accounts for about four-fifths of the value of all U.S. stocks) are distributed. Broad sectors represented about one-eighth of the S&P each: finance, health care, consumer goods (like P&G), industrial materials (chemicals, steel, etc.), consumer and business services (Walmart Stores, H&R Block), energy, computer hardware, and (as a single sector) media, telecom, and software. But be warned that the S&P's allocations can get awfully lopsided if one sector soars, as it did during the high-tech bubble.

The easiest way to achieve stock diversification is by

---

* The paper has a delightful title, "Diversification: A Bigger Free Lunch." See http://kuznets.fas.harvard.edu/~campbell/papers/diversification.pdf.

owning funds that do the allocating for you. But beware *which* fund. Fidelity Contrafund—my favorite broad-based fund of all time—rarely strays too far from the sector allocations of the market itself. Contrafund owns more than 400 stocks, and its top ten holdings represent only 30 percent of the fund's total value. More focused funds, however, concentrate their bets. Janus Forty, as the name implies, owns only forty stocks, with half its assets in the fund's top ten holdings. Compared with the market, Janus Forty gives extra weight to telecom stocks and very little weight to energy. Even more extreme is Yacktman Focused, whose top *seven* holdings account for half its value. The media sector alone represents one-fourth of its assets. All three focused funds, however, have strong track records and top ratings—five stars—from Morningstar. You can certainly own such funds—just as you can own individual stocks—but also own other funds and other stocks.

By definition, an S&P index fund will provide you with the same distribution across sectors as the market. But the S&P is weighted (that is, assets are distributed) according to the market value of each stock, so if the prices of financial stocks, for example, suddenly shoot up, they could become as much as one-third of the S&P's value—far out of line with their historical weighting. The only way to protect yourself against owning too much of what could be a bad thing is to build your *own* stock portfolio and reallocate every year.

For the sake of simplicity, you might own twenty-five stocks, with three in each of the eight sectors I listed above and one more as a wild card (to make the math easier). With $100,000 to invest, you would put $4,000 into each stock. If one stock doubles within a year, one stock falls sharply, and all the rest creep up by the same amount, you will sell part of your holdings in the high-flier and buy more of the stock that dropped. The idea is to avoid having the high-fliers account for a disproportionately lofty share of your portfolio.

You also need to diversify your stock portfolio by size. As I pointed out in Chapter 3, small-caps return more than large-caps but are also more risky. More remarkable, the success of each sector seems to run in streaks. Small-caps beat large-caps, for instance, every year from 1991 to 1994; then large-caps beat small-caps for each of the next four years; then small-caps beat large-caps for each of the next eight years. (Growth and value exhibit similar streaks.) You can't forecast how long the runs will last, but you can distribute your money across stocks of both sizes—as well as mid-caps, which, as you might suspect, fall in between in return and volatility—so that the ride is smoother.

Finally, as I stressed earlier, international diversification is now a must. Over the past two decades, there has been a tight correlation between the risks of U.S. and foreign stocks, but that's because the value of foreign stocks is concentrated in companies based in Europe and Japan, whose economies are more and more like that of the United States. Aspiring markets, however, differ sharply from markets in developed nations. In 2007, iShares MSCI Brazil Index, an ETF that tracks the Brazilian market, returned seventy-two percentage points more than the S&P 500; in 2008, the fund returned nineteen points less than the S&P; then, in 2009, some ninety-eight points more than the U.S. index. Now, *that's* divergence, and it is precisely why you need to allocate part of your portfolio to aspiring markets.

Stock diversification is not a foolproof insurance policy. In 2008, the bottom fell out of *everything*. Small-caps, large-caps, international, value, growth, tech, finance, you name it: Nearly all sectors lost about a third of their value. That's why the Margin of Safety strategy prescribes asset diversification as well as stock diversification. In the miserable stock year of 2008, the returns (price gains plus interest) of intermediate-term U.S. Treasury bonds jumped 13 percent—the biggest increase since another miserable stock year, 2000.

4. THE LITTLE THINGS COUNT

The fun part of investing is buying a stock that doubles in a month, but the significant part of investing is taking care of the little, prosaic things. They count because of the power of the EMH (in the end, a diversified portfolio will come close to performing just like the market as a whole) and of compounding over time (the phenomenon of returns on returns on returns . . .).

How much, for example, do tiny differences in mutual fund costs matter? "A lot," says the Securities and Exchange Commission. "Even small differences in fees can translate into large differences in returns over time. For example, if you invested $10,000 in a fund that produced a 10 percent annual return before expenses and had annual operating expenses of 1.5 percent, then after twenty years you would have roughly $49,725. But if the fund had expenses of only 0.5 percent, then you would end up with $60,858."*

The good news is that costs have been declining as investors have become smarter about what they buy. The flow of cash to load funds (which charge an up-front or occasionally a back-end fee in addition to a percentage of your investment each year) has been declining. Between 2002 and 2008, load funds received just $42 billion in net new investment while no-load funds received $858 billion, according to the Investment Company Institute. Meanwhile, annual fees and expenses for both groups dropped from 1.98 percent in 1990 to 0.99 percent in 2008 for stock funds and from 1.89 percent to 0.75 percent for bond funds.

---

* You can find the SEC's handy mutual fund cost calculator at: www.sec.gov/investor/tools/mfcc/get-started.htm.

Unlike other areas of endeavor, in investing you don't necessarily get what you pay for. For example, Invesco Large Cap Growth charges an expense ratio of 1.4 percent and an up-front load of 5.5 percent, yet it trailed the S&P 500 by an annual average of 5 percentage points over the ten years ending mid-October 2010. Dodge & Cox Stock, with expenses of 0.5 percent, *beat* the S&P by six points a year over the same period. More important, look at index funds like Vanguard Small Cap Index, with an expense ratio of 0.28 percent.

Studies have consistently found that it rarely makes sense to buy high-fee mutual funds. "Returns come and go," John Bogle has written, "but costs go on forever." In fact, mutual funds that charge lower fees produce higher returns over long periods. Research by CD/Wiesenberger, found that the difference in returns between low-expense and high-expense funds is more than double the difference in expenses! The best lawyers may charge the highest fees, but the best mutual funds don't. Contrafund, which over the past ten years (ending early December 2010) has beaten the S&P by an average of 5 percentage points annually and with lower risk, carries an expense ratio of just 1 percent. Bruce, a riskier small-cap fund with a spectacular record that lands it in the top 1 percent of its category for its ten-year record, charges only 0.9 percent and has just $244 million in assets. (And notice that here's another great fund which, like Yacktman, bears its founder's name.) Whether Contrafund and Bruce achieved their marks through luck or skill, it's a strangely inefficient market that prices their services at the industry average—far below many inferior performers.

The second little thing that counts is not always so little: taxes. The investor's best friend is the deferral of taxes on a retirement account. If you have to pay taxes on your capital gains, dividends, and interest each year, then there is less value left over in your account to compound. Say that state and federal taxes consume 20 percent of your returns annually, so that, instead of making 10 percent on the stock part of your portfolio, you make 8 percent. At the end of twenty years, $10,000 becomes $47,000. With taxes deferred, $10,000 becomes $67,000. Apply the 20 percent tax to the entire $67,000 and you still have $54,000 left.

And don't let retirement account contribution limits thwart you. It's not difficult to create your own tax deferral by simply allowing your capital gains to accumulate, paying taxes only on the dividends. Capital gains aren't taxed until you realize them—and then at a rate that, traditionally, has been considerably lower than the rate on ordinary income, like salary. As I write, dividends are also taxed at a lower rate than salary—and lower than interest on federal and corporate bonds as well. But it's never certain how long that lower rate—15 percent for most investors—will last.

In fact, it is the vagaries of tax laws that prevent me from laying down hard-and-fast rules—except to say that you should pay close attention to the tax effects not only of buying stocks on your own but also of buying mutual funds. The funds themselves do not pay taxes on their investments; the liabilities are passed on to investors. Since fund managers are mainly judged by one number—the before-tax return they achieve each year—they have little incentive to run their portfolios with an eye to keeping investors' taxes low. Look for funds with low turnover, an indication that they don't incur taxes for you at ordinary-income rates by selling a stock at a profit in less than a year.

It is utterly foolish to keep certain investments in a taxable account. For instance, stay away from a fund like BlackRock High Income, a high-yield (or junk) bond portfolio, which had an average yearly return of 6.1 percent before taxes and a mere 2.5 percent after taxes over ten years, according to an analysis by Morningstar. Black-Rock turns its entire portfolio over once a year, and those interest payments are taxed at the top rate.

Also, watch out for the effect of bear markets on funds. Imagine that a fund has been highly successful in previous years and has built up huge, unrealized capital gains. Then, the stock market tanks, and investors panic and demand redemptions from the fund. In order to raise cash, the fund has to dump stocks, incurring big capital gains liabilities. All current shareholders in the fund have to pay the taxes on those gains—not merely shareholders who were around when the gains were accumulated.

5. HOLD ON

When you consider the efficiency of markets and the effects of taxes, the best solution for most investors is owning a stock portfolio and sitting on it for a long, long time. I began this book by saying that an investment strategy built exclusively on buying and holding a portfolio overwhelmingly composed of stocks will fail—because investors are psychologically incapable of toughing it out during a terrible market decline and because the world is changing, politically and economically. But since bonds and hedges provide ballast for lower portfolio volatility, you can more comfortably hold onto your stocks even in bad times.

There is an inspirational story told in my previous book, *The Secret Code of the Superior Investor*, that bears repeating. Anne Schreiber, a young lawyer for the Internal Revenue Service in the 1940s, never made more than $3,150 a year (the equivalent of about $45,000 today). Still, she managed to scrape together $5,000 in savings by age fifty-one and put it into stocks. When she died, her original stake was worth an astounding $7.5 million. How did she do it? "She just held on to what she bought and never sold anything," said her broker. She went through it all: World War II, the Korean War, the Kennedy assassination, the oil embargo, the 1987 one-day crash that took stocks down by nearly one-fourth. She just held on. She did have the advantage of living until age 101, but her story reminds us of the power of minimizing taxes (she felt she had been mistreated as an IRS employee and especially enjoyed depriving the Treasury of revenue) and of compounding returns. She had a well-diversified portfolio of blue chips, but her success depended not on smart stock picks but on perseverance.

Another advantage of a buy-and-hold approach is that it relieves you of the pressure of constantly wondering when to sell. If you believe in the EMH, then today's price absorbs all possible knowledge and tomorrow's price is unknown, so selling is often a futile exercise. Say you bought IBM, not a particularly volatile stock, at $98 a share in January 2004. Shares dropped to $75 in May 2005. Time to sell? If you had, you would have missed the climb back to $98 a year and a half later and then to $130 by June 2008. Time to sell? The stock took a sickening fall to $70 by November, a loss of nearly half. Time to sell? In two years, IBM had hit an all-time high of $147. Stocks *will* fluctuate. That is their nature. Guessing a bottom or a near-bottom is simply impossible, but a sensible investor might well have decided that the decline of IBM after the collapse of Bear Stearns was unwarranted, that Mister Market had become far too gloomy. She could have bought at shares at $70 or $80 and, if she continued to believe in the bank, then again at $100. The smart investor buys a company, not a price, and sells when something important has happened within the business she owns—

its management changes, a key product fails, or there's a revelation about shady accounting—not within another company in the same sector or within the economy as a whole.

What compels investors to sell? Well, either the stock rises a great deal and they want to take profits, or the stock falls a great deal and they want to limit losses. In either case, the sale is generated by a hunch that the price will go down—either because it's too high or too low (strange that both are triggers).

But a fall in price is not determined by what went before it—any more than the chances that the next coin flip will be heads is determined by a prior string of ten tails (or ten heads) in a row. Certainly, there are reasons to sell: (1) You have lost confidence in a company's management or products or are worried about new competition, (2) you can replace one stock in your portfolio with another you like better, or (3) you need the money. Buy and hold, however, should be your default position. Ignoring this rule means confronting not just a difficult decision on when to sell but also a difficult decision on when and what to buy with the proceeds. Keep things simple.

THE 18 RULES

Now, with the five principles forming the foundation, we can get to the details of the New Rulebook for the Margin of Safety strategy, a summary of the advice I have given throughout this book.

1. **Plan.** Own a well-constructed portfolio of assets that is geared to your needs. Stocks are riskier than bonds—especially over periods of ten years and less—so the shorter your time horizon, the more bonds you need. If you are investing for retirement and have a longer time horizon, you can afford to own more stocks. Come up with a specific allocation of assets: say, 50 percent stocks, 40 percent bonds, and 10 percent hedges. Stick to the plan. Reallocate annually to keep close to the same proportions. Change it only if your needs change, not if you suddenly become worried about the prospects of stocks and bonds.

2. **Know the two kinds of risk.** When investment experts talk about risk, they usually mean volatility—especially the chances that stocks will lose value. For instance, adjusted for inflation and including dividends, the large-cap stocks of the Standard & Poor's 500 Index have declined in roughly three years out of every ten. So, judging from history, your chances of losing purchasing power with an investment in stocks in a particular year are 30 percent. But there is another kind of risk—the bolt from the blue, described by the economist Frank

Knight. It is the risk that something utterly unexpected and unquantifiable will happen: a weeks-long shutdown of markets because of a terrorist cyberattack, for example, or something we can't possibly imagine today.

3. **Lower your stock allocation.** Reduce the proportion of stocks in your portfolio and raise the share of bonds. This is the most important change from the Old Rulebook to the New. In the past, like most financial advisors, I urged a long-term portfolio that was very heavy on stocks. No longer. The Margin of Safety offers an insurance policy through a shift in the way assets are allocated: lower returns but lower risk as well. For instance, history shows that the difference in average annual returns is about one and a half percentage points between a diversified portfolio composed 90 percent of stocks and 10 percent of bonds and a portfolio split 50/50. But the difference in risk is enormous. Standard deviation, a popular risk measure, is 21 percent for the 90/10 portfolio and about half that—11 percent—for the 50/50. The worst five-year period for the 90/10 portfolio produced a total loss of 63 percent; for the 50/50 portfolio, a loss of just 15 percent. Unlike the 90/10 portfolio, the 50/50 portfolio *never* lost money in any of the seventy-five overlapping ten-year

periods since 1926, according to Morningstar. The next chapter will tell what allocation is right for you.

4. **Hedge.** Every portfolio must have hedges to protect investors, as much as possible, from both kinds of risk specified in Rule No. 2. The simplest hedge is a bear fund—a mutual fund that structures derivatives in such a way that, when the market falls, the investor benefits—and vice versa.

5. **Invest regularly.** Adding new money is even better than buying and selling stocks or bonds to maintain your allocations. That way you avoid the tax consequences. The best way to invest, if you can afford it, is regularly and automatically—with withdrawals from your salary that go each pay period, each quarter, or each year into stocks and bonds.

6. **Dividends pay.** When a stock pays a substantial dividend, management is showing its confidence that future cash flow will be strong. And when a stock pays a dividend that rises each year over long periods, it's likely that the underlying company has a "moat" that protects it from the ravages of competition on profits. Dividends are the most transparent indicator of a stock's true value, and a dividend puts cash in your pocket every quar-

ter. With all these benefits, stocks that consistently pay good dividends should be the bedrock of your portfolio.

7. **Buy aspiring nations.** You can no longer own a stock portfolio composed only of U.S. companies. You must go international, and lean heavily toward stocks of aspiring (also called developing) nations, such as India, China, and Brazil. And, when buying the stocks of these countries, look for companies that sell to the *domestic* market, rather than companies dependent on exports to more mature economies like the United States and Japan. Aspiring nations will have a significant advantage over mature economies in the years ahead. What they lack in strong governance, they will probably overcome in good demographics, a lack of legacy welfare obligations, rising levels of education, and entrepreneurial zeal.

8. **Buy micro-caps.** Always search for inefficiencies— for stocks that the market may be pricing inaccurately. One of the best places to hunt is among the smallest of the small: the micro-cap sector. Research shows clearly that small stocks return more than large, but small stocks are also more risky. With the other protections afforded by the Margin of Safety strategy, you can afford to buy micro-caps, despite their volatility.

9. **Buy value stocks.** A fruitful area of inefficiency is among value stocks, especially the extreme-value companies that Benjamin Graham, originator of the financial term *margin of safety,* prized. While Graham looked at individual companies to determine whether they were undervalued, we can see the aggregate effect of value on returns through ranking stocks by valuation measures such as book value. Defined this way, large-cap value stocks beat large-cap growth stocks in seven of the past nine decades—and by a wide margin.

10. **Index.** The easiest way to diversify is by owning index funds—either conventional mutual funds, which you buy directly through the firms that manage them or through your own investment advisor, or exchange-traded funds (ETFs) that trade on the major exchanges as if they were individual stocks. In either case, the fund's composition is based on a formula that tries to reflect a particular market or sector. The most popular index funds are based on the Standard & Poor's 500, roughly the 500 largest U.S. public companies, representing about four-fifths of the value of the stock market as a whole. But you can also buy an index fund based on the stocks of an individual nation (such as Japan) or region (Latin America) or based on the stocks of an industry (finance) or the size of

firms (small-caps) or valuation (value stocks). The "weighting" of the proportion that each stock represents in an index fund's portfolio is usually based on the stock's market capitalization (its shares outstanding multiplied by price per share). A major advantage of index funds is their low expense ratios, which usually amount to only a few tenths of a percentage point; the fund, after all, doesn't have to pay the salary of a brilliant stock picker. And, as we have seen, the brilliance of such pickers is suspect anyway. Over long periods, most index funds beat managed funds.

11. **Bonds are beautiful.** In the past, many investment advisors (me, included) looked at bonds with condescension. Now, with the devastation to stocks over the past decade, the benefits of bonds have become evident. Yes, there are risks—rising interest rates or deteriorating credit quality. And, yes, the returns of bonds have been lower historically than the returns of stocks. But, very often, when stocks are down, bonds (especially Treasuries) are up, and bonds provide a steady flow of cash. The Margin of Safety strategy urges you to: (1) "ladder" your bonds, that is, spread out their maturities so that if rates rise, you'll be able to buy higher-rate bonds with the principal you get back; (2) move beyond Treasuries and U.S. agency

bonds to high-quality corporates and municipals; (3) try to keep maturities no longer than ten years unless shorter-maturity rates are very low; and (4) seek a "5 percent solution," targeting an interest rate of about 5 percent when inflation is running in the 2–3 percent range.

12. **Take TIPS.** A special kind of Treasury bond, launched in 1997, pays a flat "real" rate of interest and then adds an inflation bonus each year based on the Consumer Price Index. For instance, a series of TIPS (standing for Treasury Inflation-Protection Securities) that matures in January 2016 carries a real rate of 2 percent. If you bought the bond when it was issued and inflation averages 2.2 percent, then the effective rate for the bond will be 4.2 percent. While TIPS aren't foolproof—their prices fluctuate for reasons that are not always understandable, so if you have to sell before maturity, you might take a loss—they are the best security against a significant rise in inflation.

13. **Go beyond the dollar.** And, speaking of currency and diversification . . . Investors need to move beyond the dollar. Your salary is paid in dollars, the value of your house is in dollars, and the companies and agencies that stand behind your stocks and bonds do business in dollars. As a typical

American, you are "long" the dollar—that is, you are heavily dependent on its retaining and increasing its value. But, in today's world, a strong dollar is no certainty. All investors need to diversify part of their portfolios out of the dollar—in part by owning foreign stocks and, in some cases, by owning funds that invest in foreign currencies.

14. **Beware of commodities.** Because the prices of many commodities have risen in the past decade—and because there is a lack of correlation between commodities and stocks—investors may be tempted to jump into the commodities futures market. Don't. Futures, which are contracts to buy or sell commodities (ranging from grains and metals and oil to meat and juice and currencies), are simply too risky for most investors. They use heavy leverage—that is, extreme levels of debt. You *can* buy unleveraged, exchange-traded notes, whose return is linked to commodity indexes, but, if you insist, I much prefer owning individual stocks in businesses like energy, precious metals, or agriculture, whose prices are mainly determined by the ups and downs of commodities. Another way to capitalize on rising commodity prices is through a fund like PIMCO Commodity Real Return Strategy, which owns a portfolio of commodities and

trades them actively. But even a respected firm like PIMCO has trouble in the commodities markets. The fund fell 44 percent in 2008 and charges expenses that are far above average. By the way, taxes on the PIMCO fund, because it trades so much, are enormous. Its stated return since inception is an average of 8.8 percent a year, but, after taxes, according to Morningstar, the return is a mere 3.6 percent.

15. **It *Is* the Economy.** In my 2002 book, *The Secret Code of the Superior Investor,* I urged readers not to worry about the economy—first, because it is unpredictable and, second, because it takes care of itself. Therefore, I argued, in a reverse play on the famous statement of political strategist James Carville, "It's *not* the economy, stupid." But the New Rulebook takes a different position. The U.S. economy may be unpredictable in the short term, but, in the long term, a prudent investor should worry about the prospects for strong, prolonged growth. The world is changing, and an economy that could be expected, despite some ups and down, to grow at 3 percent or even 4 percent, will now be fortunate to grow at 2 percent. That's a big difference over time. Your portfolio needs to change to reflect current reality—by, for instance, adding the stocks of aspiring markets and relying more heavily on bonds.

16. **Embrace Tough Times.** The payoff for successful stock investing at times of high uncertainty can be enormous. Look at World War II. After Hitler's capture of France and most of the rest of Europe, after Pearl Harbor and the early Japanese victories against the Americans, who knew where the largest conflagration in history was headed? Yet, in the four years ending December 31, 1945, the S&P, including dividends, rose 149 percent. The Margin of Safety strategy gives you the freedom and confidence to own stocks when everyone else is shunning them—as long as you continue to balance equities with bonds and hedges.

17. **You're on your own.** Don't count on Social Security: Benefits will almost certainly be reduced over the next few decades. Don't count on the financial regulators: They can't anticipate every form of chicanery. Don't count on the experts: They missed the disasters since 2000 and won't predict the next one. Your investing future is in your own hands—which is why the protection afforded by the Margin of Safety strategy is critical.

18. **Have fun.** For many, investing is a frightening, daunting, or dreary experience. It shouldn't be. Having laid down rules, I believe you can now operate as an investor with more confidence and

exhilaration than you can without knowing where you stand. Be a happy investor.

With these five principles and eighteen rules in hand, you are missing only one ingredient of the Margin of Safety strategy: specifics on how to structure your portfolio. You need to know not merely what proportion of stocks and bonds to own, but, within those large groups of assets, what proportion of international stocks, Treasury bonds, and other particulars. The final chapter provides those answers.

6

STRESS-TEST YOUR PORTFOLIO

The most important element of the Margin of Safety strategy is the way you allocate the assets in your portfolio—a big change from what many advisors (including me) advocated in the past. In this chapter, I explain in detail what your new portfolio should look like. We will explore the following:

- The proportion of stocks and bonds you should own.

- How you should divide up your money within each asset class.

- What to do about hedges and currencies.

STOCKS AND BONDS

The division between stocks and bonds depends mainly on your time horizon: how soon you need to start turning those assets into cash—for example, to send a child to college, buy a house, take a vacation, or provide for your own retirement income. If your withdrawals are far off, you can own more stocks; if they are near, own less. To make life simple, I divide withdrawal time horizons into three categories: five to ten years (medium term), ten to thirty years (long term), and more than thirty years (very long term). What about short term? If you need the money in less than five years, you shouldn't be in stocks at all; shares are just too risky in the short term, so stick to an all-bond or bond-and-cash portfolio.

For the medium-term category, divide your assets this way: 30 percent stocks, 70 percent bonds.

For long-term investors, the proportions are 50/50.

For very-long-term investors, 70 percent stocks, 30 percent bonds.

Even if you are saving only for one purpose—say, retirement—you will, of course, move from one category to the other. If you are thirty-five today and plan to retire and start withdrawals at age seventy, then you are a very long-term investor, but in five years, you will become a long-term investor and need to shift accordingly.

Now let's perform some simple stress tests on different portfolios to show their real-life effects. We'll use three representative years: 1997, when a portfolio that was fully invested in stocks (the S&P 500 index) returned 33 percent and bonds did fairly well; 2001, when stocks lost 12 percent and bonds were mediocre; and 2008, when stocks lost 37 percent and bonds returned a positive 26 percent. All the examples below involve investors with normal risk aversion. The proxy for the bond portfolio is a U.S. Treasury bond with a maturity of twenty years. Both stock and bond returns include changes in prices, plus dividends or interest.

SCENARIO 1

Very-long-term time horizon: 70 percent stocks/30 percent bonds

1997 return: 28 percent (compared with 33 percent for all stocks)

2001 return: –7 percent (compared with –12 percent for all stocks)

2008 return: –22 percent (compared with –37 percent for all stocks)

SCENARIO 2

Long-term time horizon: 50 stocks/50 bonds

1997 return: 25 percent

2001 return: –4 percent

2008 return: –10 percent

SCENARIO 3

Medium-term time horizon: 30 stocks/70 bonds

1997 return: 21 percent

2001 return: –1 percent

2008 return: 3 percent

What is so striking about these scenarios is how volatility drops when you add bonds. The difference in total returns between the all-stock portfolios in the highly profitable year (1997) and the big-loss year (2008) is 70 percentage points. But with a 50/50 portfolio, the difference is half that: just 35 percentage points.

STOCKS, BONDS, AND A HEDGE

To these simple stock-and-bond portfolios, let's now add an essential complication: the bear-fund hedge we described in Chapter 2. Now, the very-long-term investor will divide her assets this way: 60 percent stocks, 30 percent bonds, 10 percent hedge. Other portfolios also replace a one-tenth share of stocks with the bear-fund hedge, which, remember, performs in an inverse ratio with the large-cap U.S. stocks. If the S&P is up 17 percent, I will assume in these calculations that the hedge will lose 17 percent, and vice versa.

SCENARIO 4

Long-term time horizon, with hedge: 40 percent stocks, 50 percent bonds, 10 percent hedge

   1997 return: 18 percent (vs. 33 for all stocks)

   2001 return: –2 percent (vs. –12 for all stocks)

   2008 return: 2 percent (vs. –37 for all stocks)

The long-term stock/bond/hedge portfolio actually produced a positive return in 2008(!), and volatility between 1997 and 2008 decreased dramatically. The gap fell from 70 percent with an all-stock portfolio to a mere 16 percent with the 40/50/10 portfolio.

RISK-AVERSION ADJUSTMENT

The basic stock/bond/hedge portfolio is a base. You should gauge how risk-averse you are and adjust in two ways, according to your own temperament. First, if you are especially jittery about volatility, you may shift ten points of stocks into bonds. Second, if you feel you are *less* worried about risk than most investors, don't ratchet your stock proportion higher; instead, deduct your hedge from the bond, rather than the stock, part of your portfolio.

SCENARIO 5

Adjustments to the long-term portfolio and how they would have affected 2008 returns:

1. Start with the standard 50/50 stock-bond allocation (return: –10 percent).

2. Add a hedge: 40 stocks, 50 bonds, 10 hedge (return: 2 percent).

3. If you are especially risk-averse, shift ten points of stocks into the bond category, thus: 30 stocks, 60 bonds, 10 hedge (return: 8 percent).

4. If you have below-average risk aversion, take the hedge out of bonds rather than stocks, thus: 50 stocks, 40 bonds, 10 hedge (return: –4 percent).

INSIDE YOUR STOCK ALLOCATION

Now, we move to the question of how to allocate *within* each asset of the categories. Start with stocks. In the previous chapters of this book, I have recommended the following groups:

- Stocks, or stock funds, that pay consistent and fairly high dividends.

- Micro-cap stocks, or funds.

- Value stocks, or funds.

- Stocks, or stock funds, from international aspiring, or emerging, markets.

- Stocks of individual companies you know and like.

Divide the money you have allocated for stocks (not your total portfolio—just the stock part) among these five groups, according to the following rules:

1. Each of the first four groups must be represented with at least 10 percent of your stock assets, except aspiring-market stocks and funds, which should be at least 20 percent of your total value.

2. You don't have to indulge in the "stocks you know and like" category at all, but if you do, keep

it to no more than 20 percent of your total stock value.

3. No other category may represent more than 40 percent of your total stock value.

While you do have flexibility in shaping your portfolio, stick to a plan for at least five years. For both stocks and bonds, rebalancing once a year—to bring your allocations back to their starting proportions—is a requirement of the Margin of Safety strategy. (I describe how to rebalance in detail in Chapter 2.)

INSIDE YOUR BOND ALLOCATION

Let's now allocate within the category of bonds. Here are the subgroups from which you can choose individual bonds, or funds:

- Treasury bonds or federal agency bonds.
- Investment-grade (and slightly below) corporate bonds.
- TIPS: bonds whose returns are linked to inflation.
- High-quality municipal bonds.

Here are the rules for spreading your money among different kinds of bonds:

1. Munis are optional, but the other three groups must be represented.

2. At least 20 percent of your bond portfolio must be in TIPS.

3. Between 30 percent and 50 percent must go to corporates.

4. If you own individual bonds, you should ladder maturities so that roughly 10 percent of your portfolio matures each year.

5. Maturities may stretch from two to thirty years. Your aim should be to produce a 5 percent yield when inflation is in a range of 2 to 3 percent, and higher if inflation is higher.

6. If you own bond funds instead of individual bonds, be sure that roughly two-thirds of your holdings are in short- or medium-term funds (with maturities averaging five to ten years).

OPTIONAL

You may put up to 5 percent of your total stock/bond/hedge portfolio into each of these investments:

- Currency hedges. You may buy funds that invest in foreign currencies or in bonds denominated in foreign currencies, especially those of developing markets, as I described in Chapter 4.

- A fun-and-games account. Many investors simply can't sit still. The best way to handle the urge to trade is by confining it to a small amount of money. Within that small amount, you may buy and sell stocks to your heart's content.

- Cash, by which I mean money market funds, short-term certificates of deposit, or savings accounts.

MARGIN OF SAFETY VERSUS CONTROL

Now, let's look at a detailed sample portfolio. (I have appended dividend yields for stocks, as of early December 2010.)

Total portfolio value: $1 million. Summary: stocks 45 percent, hedges and currencies 15 percent, bonds 40 percent.

STOCKS

DIVIDEND STOCKS AND FUNDS, $150,000

Chubb, insurance (yield: 2.5 percent), $10,000

Cintas, work uniforms (1.7 percent), $10,000

Enterprise Products Partners, LP, energy (5.8 percent), $10,000

Merck, pharmaceuticals (4.3 percent), $10,000

Clorox, household products (3.5 percent), $10,000

SPDR S&P Dividend (ETF), $50,000

Vanguard Dividend Appreciation (ETF), $50,000

VALUE STOCK STOCKS AND FUNDS, $100,000

Overseas Shipholding, bulk shipping (4.8 percent), $10,000

Atrion, medical devices (1 percent), $10,000

Bank of America (0.3 percent), $10,000

Pepsico, consumer products (3 percent), $10,000

Washington Post, media and education (2.3 percent), $10,000

Yacktman Fund, $20,000

iShares Morningstar Large Value Index (ETF), $20,000

Weitz Value Partners (mutual fund), $10,000

DEVELOPING MARKETS STOCKS AND FUNDS, $100,000

Petrobras Energía, Brazil energy (2.6 percent), $10,000

Ctrip International, China travel services, $10,000

America Movil, Mexico telecom (0.4 percent), $10,000

HDFC Bank, India financial (0.4 percent), $10,000

Banco Bradesco, Brazil financial (0.5 percent), $10,000

SPDR S&P Emerging Markets Small Cap (ETF), $10,000

China Fund (closed-end fund), $10,000

India Fund (closed-end fund), $10,000

Vanguard Emerging Markets Stock Index (mutual fund), $20,000

MICRO-CAP STOCK FUNDS, $100,000

Aegis Value (mutual fund), $50,000

Bridgeway Ultra-Small Company Market (mutual fund), $50,000

BONDS

TREASURY INFLATION-PROTECTION SECURITIES (TIPS) AND FUNDS, $100,000

TIPS 1.25 percent (real return) of 2020, $30,000

TIPS 2.5 percent of 2029, $30,000

Vanguard Inflation Protected Securities (mutual fund), $40,000

U.S. TREASURIES AND AGENCIES, $100,000

PIMCO 3–7-Year Treasury Index (ETF), $30,000

Fidelity Government Income (mutual fund), $30,000

Vanguard Intermediate Term Bond Index (ETF), $40,000

CORPORATES, $200,000

Fidelity Capital & Income (mutual fund), $30,000

T. Rowe Price Short-Term Bond (mutual fund), $30,000

PIMCO Investment Grade Corporate Bond* (mutual fund), $40,000

---

* The PIMCO fund includes foreign bonds, giving investors some diversification out of the dollar.

American Express Bank 3.1 percent of 2011*, $10,000

Sprint Capital 8.4 percent of 2012, $10,000

Hewlett Packard 4.5 percent of 2013, $10,000

Morgan Stanley 6 percent of 2014, $10,000

HCP 6 percent of 2015, $10,000

Anandarko Petroleum 6 percent of 2016, $10,000

Bank of America 5.3 percent of 2017, $10,000

AmerenEnergy Generating 7 percent of 2018, $10,000

CSX 7.4 percent of 2019, $10,000

Goldman Sachs 6 percent of 2020, $10,000

HEDGES AND CURRENCIES

BEAR FUND, $100,000

ProShares Short S&P 500 (ETF), $100,000

---

* This bond and the nine that follow provide "laddering," or maturities in successive years, a technique described in Chapter 4. The interest rates listed are commitments of companies when the bonds were issued. As I write in late 2010, all of these bonds are traded at a premium, which means that investors pay more than face value, so the bonds carry a lower yield than the coupon. For instance, the Hewlett Packard 2013 bond yields 1 percent, and the Goldman Sachs 2020 bond yields 4.6 percent. Check prevailing yields with a broker or online before you buy.

CURRENCY FUNDS, $50,000

WisdomTree Dreyfus Emerging Currency Fund (ETF), $20,000

CurrencyShares Japanese Japanese Yen Trust (ETF), $10,000

CurrencyShares Euro Trust (ETF), $20,000

SCENARIO 6

In 2008, the portfolio's dividend stocks* lost 23 percent, for a loss of $40,000. Value stocks lost 36 percent, for a loss of $36,000. Developing markets lost a hefty 53 percent, for a loss of $53,000. And micro-caps were down 41 percent, for a loss of $41,000.

The bear-fund hedge gained 39 percent, for a profit of $39,000. The currency funds rose about 5 percent, for a gain of $3,000.

As for the bond portion of the portfolio . . . TIPS returned 1 percent, for a gain of $1,000; Treasuries and agencies were up 8 percent, including both price rises and interest, for $8,000; and corporates picked up 2 percent, for a gain of $4,000.

So, overall, stocks lost $170,000, hedges and curren-

---

* In order for this analysis to be meaningful (I could have cheated by picking stocks that went way up), relevant index funds and ETFs, rather than individual stocks, bonds, and managed funds, were used in these calculations.

cies gained $42,000, and bonds gained $13,000. Net loss: $115,000, or 12 percent.

Now, let's compare with a Control Portfolio—that is, the sort of portfolio that most financial advisors tend to recommend: 80 percent stocks, divided among a large-cap growth index fund (50 percent), an international fund (15 percent), and a total-U.S.-market fund that includes small- and mid-cap stocks in addition to large-caps (15 percent). These funds together produced a loss of $312,000, or nearly 40 percent. The bond portion, comprising 15 percent Treasuries and 5 percent TIPS, returned about $13,000, or 7 percent.

So, here is the result for 2008: Detailed Margin of Safety Portfolio (45 stocks/40 bonds/10 bear-fund hedge/5 currencies): 12 percent loss.

Control Portfolio (80/20): 30 percent loss.

Certainly, not every year will be like 2008, but if another 2008 comes along, the Margin of Safety strategy protects you against catastrophic losses. If history repeats itself over the longer term, then, by adopting the approach laid out in this book, you will achieve annual returns that average about 8 percent, rather than about 10 percent with an all-stock portfolio. In other words, a sacrifice of a few points protects you against the horrors that can befall your portfolio through conventional investing—horrors that will inevitably come again because the world is changing.

The economic forces that kept the U.S. economy growing powerfully during most of the post–World War II period are being constrained by headwinds—caused by the enormous debt load acquired by Americans and their government, by demographic imbalances, and by decadence and a lack of political will. Meanwhile, the chances of bolts from the blue—calamities which, like 9/11, we cannot possibly predict—are growing.

Those headwinds may dissipate. Fears of Knightian disaster may be overblown. And the U.S. economy may bounce back with policies that encourage "a 4 percent solution" of robust GDP growth. It could happen. But if the financial world develops so happily, you will be benefiting in other ways: You'll get raises, and your house will appreciate in value. And your portfolio will do awfully well, too.

To invest with confidence—in fact, to *live* with confidence—you need a safety net that's there to catch you if you fall, whether it ever has to save you or not.

ACKNOWLEDGMENTS

This is a short book, but it was hard to write because it involved a change of mind and a change of heart.

Certainly, the events of the past eleven years helped alter my views, but just as important was what I believe is a better ability to see the world in shades not just of rose but of gray, taupe, and sea foam—as well as a better ability to empathize with the personal struggles of investors. For all this, I have many people to thank, notably Warren Poland.

Inspiration and encouragement (as well as the title itself!) came from my wife, Beth, the love of my life. Rafe Sagalyn, my literary agent for twenty-five years, not only did what agents normally do but also critically shaped this book as it went through several iterations. John Mahaney of Crown Business, who has edited all three of my efforts, was the soul of perspicacity and kindness. Thanks as well to my editor at *Kiplinger's Personal Finance*, Manny Schiffres, and to those who have aided through the years in my financial education, especially Ian Arnof, Kevin Hassett, and David Fenstermaker.

INDEX